Secrets of the Blue Ridge

STORIES FROM WESTERN ALBEMARLE

PHIL JAMES

Phil James

WHITE HALL MEDIA

STORIES FROM WESTERN ALBEMARLE

Book layout and cover design by Allie Marshall Pesch

Printed on acid-free paper in the United States of America

Library of Congress Control Number: 2010939952

First published 2010

10 9 8 7 6 5 4 3 2 1

WHITE HALL MEDIA
P. O. Box 88
White Hall, VA 22987
www.WhiteHallMedia.com

Edition ISBNs
    Softcover   978-1-936518-52-4
    Hardcover   978-1-936518-53-1

Stories in this book previously appeared in the *Crozet Gazette*.

Front cover image:
Steam locomotive emerging from the eastern portal of Col. Claudius Crozet's Blue Ridge Tunnel, beneath Rockfish Gap near Afton, Virginia, c.1910. Image from a vintage hand-colored postcard in the author's collection.

Back cover images:
(Top) The old springhouse as viewed from the kitchen window of the former Paul Clayton cabin in Brown's Cove, Virginia. Photo by the author.
(Bottom) Apple grading and packing crew, c.1935, at Walnut Level Farm near Mount Fair, Virginia. Original photograph from the author's collection.

This work is dedicated to my Lord and Savior, Jesus Christ,
with gratitude for allowing me this very rewarding season of my life.
Galatians 2:20

To my wife Sally, my helpmate in all things,
and to Susie Pearle ~
two demonstrations of God's marvelous gift of grace in my life;

… and to all those who have welcomed me into their homes
and confirmed, time and again, that everybody has a piece of the story.

Contents

Author's Preface

These Secrets of the Blue Ridge stories are the result of my pursuing a desire to connect with my own family's past. Lists of genealogical names, dates and places couldn't tell me who my ancestors really were. I yearned to know the life experiences masked by that proverbial "dash" between their birth and death dates. And who were the neighbors? Where did they attend school and church? At whose store did they trade? Sure, they worked hard, but what did they do for fun?

As far back in my family's history as I've been able to peer, it seems I'm the first in that long line who didn't spend a considerable portion of his or her life as a farmer. By the close of World War II, my Daddy had moved his young family into the city where he labored to make what he believed at the time was a better life for himself and his own.

Every Sunday after church, though, the entire family was "back home" in the country. Siblings and cousins faithfully gathered there for Sunday dinner and the chance to catch up on everyone else's news. Familiar stories were told again and again, traditions were kept, and many of the life patterns of our ancestors were preserved.

That cozy, familiar world changed, however, shortly before I was born. The orchards which my grandfather had managed for decades were sold and, soon thereafter, Grandmother passed away. Granddaddy moved away from the old home place and, at an advanced age, took a job in a saw mill, enduring the labor demands expected of much younger men, in order to be listed on the ledgers of a new government program called Social Security.

Momma's siblings had already departed the foothills for regular paychecks in industrial factories on both sides of the Blue Ridge Mountains. My Granny, a.k.a. Mam-maw, after spending her life making a home for her eight children, was moved out of the country into town to live with one of them.

My own growing-up years in the 1950s were typical of the narrow focus of a child and relatively free of care. So when the irrepressible call descended upon me years later to "put down on paper" the stories of my family, I realized that I had not paid good attention to the story-gifts I had surely been offered during those formative years. Oh, there were a few home sites and small villages where I could note my ancestors had once lived, and simple remembrances of favorite aunts and uncles whose occasional overnight visits required me to give up "my" room. But severely lacking was a ready archive of stories of these lives.

A breakthrough of sorts came when I was offered the opportunity to copy a quantity of old photographs from a family whose last local member had recently passed away. What I discovered was a treasure trove of images, not only of the family of the deceased, but also of several generations-worth of their neighbors. Few were identified, but it was obvious that they had been residents of the local community.

After printing the photos and mounting some on display boards and others in albums, I began to listen-up for opportunities to share them. Apple butter boilin's, church homecomings, family reunions, community picnics—word slowly got around about what I was trying to accomplish. Invitations into the homes of my neighbors followed, and as I shared the pictures I had found, they, in turn, shared from their own albums. As faces were recognized and identities recorded, reminiscences poured forth.

In 2002, by the pure grace of God and with the love and support of my wife Sally, a family decision was made that I should step away from my "day job" in order to have greater flexibility to make visits and gather recollections while they could still be had.

The shared stories and photos of people and places within our mountain and piedmont region began to reveal the tapestry of community which I had been seeking. In 2003 and 2004, Brian Cohen, then editor of *The Whistle: The Voice of Western Albemarle,* allotted space in his publication where I could begin to reach out via a monthly column, and Secrets of the Blue Ridge was born.

The Crozet Gazette was established in 2006, and, with Editor Mike Marshall's encouragement, an expanded Secrets of the Blue Ridge column reached out to an even wider audience, at home and online. Additional photos added to the stories' appeal, and reader response motivated further research and writing.

The agrarian lifestyle in central Virginia's Blue Ridge Mountains has undergone significant economic and cultural changes in recent decades. Many current residents of the western slopes of Albemarle County, as well as neighbors in Augusta, Greene, Nelson and Rockingham Counties, are as likely as not to trace their ancestral roots to these hills and valleys. These selections from previously published Secrets of the Blue Ridge are shared with the hope that we each may come to identify with and celebrate our shared heritage in this beautiful place.

Introduction

Whenever someone begins to compliment the *Crozet Gazette*, I know Phil James and his Secrets of the Blue Ridge column will be mentioned in the next sentence. Lo, it has happened thus so many times.

The first thing readers marvel over are the stare-inducing photographs he manages to find. Next is his avuncular style, so sympathetic to the lives of those who have been here before us, and often trailing a moral. His column runs towards the front of the newspaper because we know readers can't wait to get to it.

A tactful and disarming interviewer who honors confidences, Phil gets around to visiting elders, taking down their stories, and preserving their photographs. To gaze on these, with their plain truths, and to listen to those voices, is to become humbled by our ancestors, for what they endured, what they achieved and what they bequeathed to us. That is a good point to make, given how ready we are to think the world was not here before we were.

In a vivid detail, a telling fact, Phil gives us precious glimpses of the people who once shared our Blue Ridge vistas. We have been here now for many generations—Phil is on to the primacy of families—and when we follow his inviting hand, the legacies of past lives come into full view.

MICHAEL J. MARSHALL
EDITOR, *THE CROZET GAZETTE*

1

Front Porch Investments

Storefront porches such as A. C. Bruce's, adjacent to the C&O Depot in Greenwood, Virginia, were often used by merchants to display their durable wares. Local news was frequently exchanged there by neighbors, and, occasionally, a glimpse of the outside world was gleaned from rail passengers during a stopover. [Photo courtesy of Pete McCauley.]

Hey, want to hear a sure-fire way to increase your personal worth? Invest in some front porches! Now, don't scoff at the idea right off—folks have been doing it for ages and reports abound on the great returns realized. Just read on.

Okay, first off, we're not talking decks or patios here, though they have their own sets of advantages. Nor those little stoops where there's just room enough to wipe your feet before you step inside. No, we're talking plain ol' covered porches on the front side of the house. They need to be big enough for a few people to sit around—preferably on rockers—but stools, benches, gliders, mule-ear'd chairs, sofas or even La-Z-Boys will do. Now, here's the best news of all—if the house you're living in doesn't have one, you can realize the same return by investing in your neighbor's front porch. Just make sure they're "investing" at the same time. It'll double the return.

Front porches. Just think of all the history that's made right there: kids heading out to their

Woodrow Keyton and his neighbor Alton Morris often sat down together on Keyton's porch near White Hall to reminisce, talk weather, and otherwise enjoy one another's friendship.

first day of school, or a first date, or off to military service. They are places we dash to when it rains, or retreat to when it's hot. It's where company gets welcomed by the family dog, where paper boys tested their aim, and the milk man once made his early-morning exchanges.

During America's post-WWII love affair with highway travel, motor courts provided porch-like extensions and outdoor chairs for their guests' relaxation. And at least one major restaurant chain today still markets their image of a front porch lined with over-sized rocking chairs.

Front porches were the original neighborhood-watch headquarters. Gardeners, with aprons donned, settled down there to snap beans or shell peas. In towns they were sometimes pulpits for announcements, or, occasionally, court facilities for the local justice-o'-the-peace.

Porches were placed where the house faced the community. Always they were places of rest and retreat, where families and neighbors greeted one-another with a wave of the hand or the wagging of an ever-present flyswatter.

On a late summer afternoon in 1985, this writer, accompanied by his cousin Virginia Baptist "Bap" (Sandridge) Hicks, enjoyed a front porch visit with Bap's McAllister kinfolk, Cecil and Mertie. The McAllister siblings' ancestral home sat on a knoll above the first bridge into Sugar Hollow. Unmarried, they had lived their entire lives together in the same weather-boarded log cabin where they had been born: Mertie May, the third of seven children, in 1899; and Cecil, the youngest, in 1913.

Introductions included familiar recitations all around of kinship strings. Soon, however, separate but simultaneous conversations by the "men folk" and the "women folk" commenced on either end of the porch, while each party kept one ear casually attuned to the other party's train of conversation.

Cousin Bap loved people and folks loved her in return. She was probably the best in this particular grouping at keeping up closely with both conversations. During one rare lull, she commented across the porch to me, "They had a crippled brother."

Bill McAllister (1897–1964), also unmarried, spent most of his life on wooden crutches. His strong, handsome features were prominent in a rich store of family photos: in studio shots, at neighborhood functions, laboring in his older brother's sawmill. Bill was even known to drive the family truck into the village on occasion. In his latter years he was more often recalled sitting on the front porch watching the traffic on the road below.

Mertie: "When Bill was six years old, he had the infantile paralysis."

Bap: "He used to sit right there and count the cars when cars first commenced going up in Sugar Hollow so much."

Cecil: "He'd count 'em the first day of fishing season. He was busy then!"

Mertie: "It was over 300 come by here that day."

Cecil: "That many now and it ain't even fishing season."

As shadows lengthened across the yard and silent pauses in the conversations became more noticeable, the evening sounds mingled with those of the river below. Bap asked about the old family burying ground, and Cecil offered a walk up the hill behind the house to the private graveyard.

Along the way we passed the site of an earlier detached kitchen. "We had to go away from home to cook and eat," Cecil said with a grin. "Lot of old houses built like that, you know."

Walking back down the ridge from the cemetery, a wooded area was pointed out that once had been a productive apple orchard. Once-cultivated fields where wheat, corn and oats had been raised lay hidden on the hillside now populated with middle-aged trees. Our stroll ended back at

Cecil and Mertie McAllister relished the chance to relax from the day's tasks on their porch overlooking Moorman's River and the road into Albemarle County's Sugar Hollow. The siblings' guest on this occasion was their cousin Bap Hicks.

Mary Jane and Sam Garrison, accompanied by their collie dog, relax together during the heat of a summer day. Their cabin home and surrounding farm was situated on the eastern face of Pasture Fence Mountain. The Garrison's front porch offered an unexcelled view of the rolling piedmont. [Photo courtesy of Woodrow and Rosie Keyton.]

Lillie Batten Coleman stands with a group of children on her front porch steps near Brown's Cove. Over the years, she and her husband Moses Coleman provided shelter and nurture to scores of foster children at their home in the Blue Ridge foothills of western Albemarle County. [Photo courtesy of Eldon and Mary Morris.]

Front porches have long been used as impromptu photo studios. L–R: Marion Davis, Miss Lucy Luck, Clara & Joe Ballard. Pets were usually assured a welcome to these outdoor venues. [Photo courtesy of Thelma Wyant.]

the front porch where it had begun.

After goodbyes were exchanged and we turned out of the driveway onto the highway, Bap looked over and said, "This reminded me of one time I went down to Hopewell to see Cousin Taft. We dug up everybody that had ever died." Our laughter carried us the rest of the way back to Crozet.

Even though that visit took place nearly a quarter-century ago, memories remain ever-fresh of the voices and pleasant sounds carried on the breezes of that special evening. Priceless time spent—no, invested—on a front porch.

Daily National Intelligencer.

WASHINGTON: THURSDAY, JANUARY 10, 1850.

TO CONTRACTORS.

BLUE RIDGE TUNNEL.—The contractor for the Blue Ridge Tunnel having failed to come forward and comply with his engagements, notice is hereby given that Proposals will again be received at the Office of the Board of Public Works, until the 21st January, 1850, for the construction of the Tunnel and approaches.

The Tunnel will be 4,260 feet long, 21 feet high, and 16 feet wide, with a ditch on each side : it will pass 700 feet under the top of the mountain and decline from west to east at the rate of 70 feet to the mile. The approaches will be in the aggregate about 2,000 feet long, and consist of deep cuts, high embankments, some walling and bridging.

Proposers who have not already examined the localities will do well to call at the office of the Engineer, on the spot, where they will obtain all necessary information.

The payments will be CASH, with a reservation of 20 per cent. until the entire completion of the work ; besides which, the contractor is required by law to give bond, with satisfactory bond and security in Virginia. The amount of the bond required will be thirty thousand dollars.

The best testimonials and an energetic prosecution of the work are expected : the contract and bond to be executed within *ten days* after the letting, and the work to begin *bona fide* within sixty days after the same period.

C. CROZET,
Engineer Blue Ridge Railroad.

Forms of proposals and specifications may be obtained at both offices.   dec 24—dt18thJ

2

Some News from Home ...for A Change

There was a rumor circulating a few weeks back that a fellow was going to start a new newspaper called *The Crozet Gazette* in our end of Albemarle County, and I thought to myself, well, it's about time. It sure would be nice to get some news from home for a change. Now, don't get me wrong. I'm not intentionally knocking the other papers around the area. You can occasionally glean some local tid-bits from them. And I would be remiss if I didn't acknowledge the consistent efforts of Jim Crosby, editor of *The Bulletin*, published in Crozet for over ten years in the 1970s and '80s. A perusal through those past issues was a reminder of a community's voice, too long silent.

Hearing about this newspaper start-up put me in the mind to dig back into some of the old papers I've accumulated over the years. One of the older papers in the stack was a copy of the Washington, D. C. *Daily National Intelligencer* from January of 1850. Buried on the back page was a request for proposals from C. Crozet, Engineer, Blue Ridge Railroad. He was looking for a contractor to construct a tunnel 4,260 feet long "under the top of the mountain". This was apparently a second chance opportunity for some qualified businessman since the original contractor had "failed to come forward and comply with his engagements". I wondered if the folks from home had to chance upon this issue just to learn why there was a delay in getting started on digging the tunnel.

A little farther down in the paper pile was a report published autumn 1856 from Charles Ellet, the Civil Engineer on the Blue Ridge Railroad project, detailing how he had designed and built the Mountain Top Track across the summit of the Blue Ridge at Rockfish Gap. For 2 ½ years this temporary track had handled eight train passages a day, moving passengers, baggage and freight from east-to-west and west-to-east. Just once during that period of time had these regular trips been thwarted: "During the last severe winter, when the travel upon all the railways of Virginia and the Northern and Western states was interrupted… for days in succession", there had been only one day the engines had failed to take the mail through "when the train was caught in a snow drift near the summit of the mountain". Ellet's report was published almost a year later in a London edition of *The Civil Engineer and Architect's Journal*. Again, I wondered to myself why we couldn't have learned this "news" from a source just a little closer to home.

Later that same year, Washington's *National Intelligencer* (the word "Daily" had been dropped from the earlier masthead) carried on its front page a note from "Mr. Crozet, the engineer of the [Blue Ridge Tunnel] work". It was a rebuttal to his critics who had claimed that the unfinished tunnel was "too small to admit the passage of the cars". Certainly his valuable time could have been better spent doing the work he had been charged with, instead of having to reply to wags a hundred miles away who had never been on the jobsite. They surely would have gotten more accurate information if they could have just read the news from home.

Eventually, as we all know (yep, read it in the paper), the tunnel and railroad were completed. However, the work would not stay in good repair for very long. The next paper I picked up had a local map prominently displayed on the front page with very recognizeable place-names: Brown's Gap; Millington; Jarman's Gap; Mechum's River; Ivy; Greenwood; Rockfish Gap. Dated October of 1864, it reported that a couple of Union generals named Sheridan and Custer had just routed Confederate General Jubal Early from the Shenandoah Valley. It seemed that Early and a few of his officers had narrowly escaped capture and had passed right through our locale during their flight east. There was a lot of news from a very biased perspective pertaining to the Union Army, and it was then that I noticed that I was looking at *The New York Herald*. New York! Have mercy on us all. The source for "local" news had gone from bad-to-worse! Even worse yet was the reporting of a travesty on our good neighbors in the Shenandoah Valley: General U. S. Grant had issued the following order which was already being carried out by General Custer: "Do all the damage you can to the railroad and crops. Carry off stock of all descriptions and negroes, so as to prevent further planting. If the war is to last another year let the Shenandoah Valley remain a barren wasteland… It is further given out that General Grant has ordered the above to be so completely carried out that a crow, flying over the valley will have to carry its own rations." So… there went our new railroad and, worse yet, our neighbors over the hill were enduring the severe hardships of war. We sure didn't need a New York newspaper telling us *that* bit of news.

The war finally ended. The railroad's tracks and burned depots were rebuilt and served as valuable links between our neighborhood and many points east and west for the next 80 years.

The last two newspapers in my stack detailed how time and "progress" can change even the grandest of man's works. In late 1941, the *Richmond Times-Dispatch* devoted a full page to "Sidetracking Crozet's Tunnel". Modern trains had eventually become too large to navigate safely Mr. Crozet's engineering marvel under the mountain top. Steps were being taken to replace the original bore with a new, larger tunnel. That "new" Blue Ridge Tunnel was completed and is still in use today.

Fast-forwarding ahead to 2006, we find *The Daily Progress* of Charlottesville reporting on yet another development. Crozet's old hand-drilled relic, after 65 years of neglect, has partially filled with water and mud, but several groups are coordinating efforts and resources hoping to re-open the 1850's tunnel to foot traffic.

Whatever the future will hold concerning these ongoing efforts, we can now rest assured that there will be a welcome, local perspective on the latest developments. Best wishes for success go out to Mike Marshall and *The Crozet Gazette*. Thanks for letting us know *the news from home!*

3
Tales of the Hunt

At this fox hunting exhibition at Pharsalia in Nelson County, it was hard to tell who was having the most enjoyable time: the excited dog pack or the nattily-attired riders.

"It's the most fun that's in the mountains."

So began an animated string of recollections by the late James Blackwell of White Hall on one of his favorite pastimes—hunting.

For some, hunting is a solitary pursuit: a time to retreat into the natural world, enjoy its solitude, and match wits with the creatures that know its rules the best.

Others anticipate the camaraderie and relative safety of participating with like-minded friends. Whether in exclusive hunting lodges with wait staff or snuggled into a converted school bus, after a day in the outdoors, few things soothe and satisfy like the scent of wood smoke, a fresh pot of hot coffee and some simmering game stew.

Hunting circles tend to be rather exclusive. There are good friends, and then there are *best*

Sugar Hollow native Bennie Blackwell was "a great turkey hunter" according to his brother Jim Blackwell. [Photo courtesy of the McAllister collection.]

friends—those that go by only one name like Peewee, Traveler, Driver, Rambler, Abe and Jack.

"Or Dave—the best fox dog that ever dropped the nose on the ground," accorded Steward Walton. "You talk about a dog… he had an unusual note on him when he barked. You could tell him in any pack."

Fox hunting is often associated today with fine horsemanship and an etiquette of prescribed attire and titled staff. But it was also enjoyed by earlier sportsmen at a time when boundary fences were erected primarily to keep stock in place rather than to bar ingress from neighbors.

Walton continued, "I can remember fox hunting and riding horses across Pasture Fence Mountain with Daddy, Mahone Madison, Tyler Wood and all of 'em. You could get out in those mountain fields and look clean off to the Sugar Hollow Road. I loved that fox hunting!"

Of course, there are always the tales, more or less the truth, repeated again and again at country stores or across the lunch table at workplaces. Tales of the hunt: the physical hardships, freezing temperatures, near misses and the ones that cleanly got away.

Several years ago, Albemarle native Jimmy Daughtry spoke in his Waynesboro home about Sugar Hollow old-timer (1867–1946) Lem James:

"Uncle Lem told me he and another fellow went bear hunting way late in the evening and treed a bear. Done got so dark they couldn't see him but they knew he was up in the tree. The other guy said, 'We're gonna have to leave him.' Lem said, 'I ain't leaving. I'm going to stay right here and get that bear.' It got chilly and he built a fire under the tree and laid down and went to sleep with the bear up over him. I'd have been scared to death, but he wasn't. He said he was just sound asleep and all at once about daylight he heard something—said that bear jumped out right in front of him and took off. And then he didn't get him! I said, man, you wouldn't have caught me sleeping with that bear over me."

In his book *From Saddle to City*, Rev. D. G. C. Butts, a minister with a circuit of seven Methodist churches in western Albemarle County from 1896–1898, wrote his lasting impression of one of his parishioners:

"Up in the very heart of the Blue Ridge in Sugar Hollow, near the head of Moorman's River, lived Oscar Early, a great bodied, big hearted mountaineer. He could entertain by the hour with miraculous stories of mountain adventure, hair-breadth escapes from bears and wild-cats, and the successful chase of the hundred different kinds of varmints that infest those parts… till one almost feared to go out of his home again lest one should be overtaken by one or more of these dreadful creatures.

"Oscar Early was my friend and brother. His home suited me, his food suited me, his cold spring water and milk suited me. His yarns held me spell-bound by day, and helped me to dream some wonderful dreams at night. His beds were what the weary body needed after a tramp over those hills."

There was a time when most every head of a household out in the country was a hunter. Whether in pioneering days, to provide his family's sustenance, or, in latter times, to supplement his table seasonally, his trusty gun's barrel was kept clean and his powder and shot were stored in a safe, dry place.

James Blackwell was affectionately called "Blackie" by those in his World War II outfit to whom he administered first aid.

"I've had blistered-up feet on might near every one of those guys," he recalled. "I was a medical aide."

He also remembered his intimacy with the Blue Ridge Mountains where he grew up. "Course I know every foot of that mountain. Stomped it with my bare toes on 'bout every rock up there when I was a boy."

Mr. Blackwell was quick to warn, though, that in *his* preferred style of hunting—rattlesnake hunting—keeping one's mind focused was paramount to a successful hunt.

"You just keep your mind exactly on the snake. You don't think about Tom, Dick and Harry and here and yonder and everywhere else. You've got your mind on one thing: that's watch where you're putting your feet. Make sure that when you see him move you're ready for him.

Hunted by some and protected by others, the venomous rattlesnake is respected by all who step foot into its domain. [Photo by V. L. James, Crozet.]

A fine evening had been spent in the 1950s by this coon hunter, equipped with a shotgun and kerosene lantern, and in the company of his two "best friends." [Photo courtesy of the Fred Morris family.]

Western Albemarle orchardist John L. James with his coon dogs, c. mid-1940s.

Fellow sportsmen gathered in White Hall with the Steppe brothers, well-known local bear hunters, when David Steppe checked in his first bear.

"I used to use a .22 all the time. I let some get away from me in briar patches, where them .22's didn't have the power to go in there and talk to 'em. Now, when I go, I carry a .357 with shot in it, plus a .22. If he's out in the open, I use the .22 on him—ain't quite as expensive as the .357. But now, if he's in the stickers or something-or-'nother, briars or weeds or grass or what-have-you, I just pull that .357 out and he goes to sleep. We've hunted them things for years."

Key to a successful hunt is scouting the area to know the types of game for which to be prepared. William Warrick sent a brief postcard message from Crozet in December 1911 to a friend in Pennsylvania. He wrote, "Some hunting here, turkeys, pheasants, quail, squirrels, etc. Saw 5 wild turkeys today, dead however. One man claims to have killed 22 this fall."

And that was probably the truth, more or less.

Tales of the Hunt by Phil James was award the Bob Gooch Outdoor Column Writing Award for 2009 by the Virginia Outdoor Writers Association. The award honors the memory of Bob Gooch, known as the Dean of Virginia Outdoor Writers, whose syndicated column "Virginia Afield" once appeared in 25 newspapers across the state.

He Who Seeks Not to Serve Others, Serves Himself Poorly

Well-baby clinics, sponsored by the County Child Welfare Committee, regularly took place in the Woman's Club clubhouse. Crozet's Dr. E. D. Davis Jr. was the attending physician at these events. [Photo courtesy of the Woman's Club of Crozet.]

In 1938 by a young man named Wallace S. Jones penned this personal philosophy: "*He who seeks not to serve others, serves himself poorly.*" I never knew Mr. Jones personally, but I've talked with several folks who knew him quite well.

His motto came to mind recently as I sorted through a box of musty papers I purchased at a local estate sale. A "Community Welfare League" had been organized in Alberene, one of our small southern Albemarle villages, in the early 1930s. Compassionate citizens banded together to

YOU HELP KEEP CROZET CLEAN

SEE USE TRASH CANS FOR PAPER

WOMANS CIVIC CLUB OF CROZET

Posters were displayed in the windows of businesses in Crozet in 1948 to encourage community pride through the use of waste receptacles placed around town. [Photo courtesy of the Woman's Club of Crozet.]

meet some of the needs of their less-fortunate neighbors. The dusty bundle included desperate notes penciled by mothers and fathers during our nation's Great Depression. There are glimpses of penniless families, hungry and in arrears at their local grocery store. Their rural neighbors were also struggling and could not help. They needed food. Their children needed clothing. Schoolteachers reported pupils who had no shoes to wear as winter approached. Mothers asked for covers for the bare beds in their rented houses. Fathers, ashamedly, confessed that they could not find enough work to provide for their families.

Concerned citizens discreetly joined with businesses, donating money and goods to meet some of the needs that were overwhelming their neighbors and threatening their community. Fundraising socials were organized. Clothing manufacturers and shoe repairmen were contacted, and reduced prices were arranged for those necessities. A local hotel prepared hundreds of bowls of soup to feed the children who arrived at school too often without a lunch.

The ledgers of those quiet endeavors were kept tucked away, but now bear witness to what being in community really means. Countless kindnesses performed by compassionate individuals helped to ease that community through those dark days.

The point came home again as I recently perused early records of *The Woman's Club of Crozet* – an organization with a wonderful record of service within the Crozet community. There I learned of the first library in Crozet, established in 1908. It was supported by membership dues and book donations. From this early library organization emerged, in 1920, a service organization called *The Woman's Civic Club of Crozet*. It described itself as "a benign leaven in a growing, complex community."

Promoting civic pride was a paramount aim of early club members. "Waste receptacles" were placed around town to control litter, and the club then paid for its removal. They "dissuaded the C&O Railway from putting up an ugly coal house in the town square," and their "repeated appeals resulted in 1924 in a new depot with landscaped grounds."

Their numerous school projects included the installation of a flagpole at Crozet High School and the establishment of that school's first library. They provided for hot soup and cocoa to students twice a week during the coldest winter months, and sponsored prizes for student essays on "How Our Town Can Be Improved." The Woman's Club clubhouse on Carter Street was used to host well-baby clinics by the County Child Welfare Committee.

Other acts of community involvement were less public. Reflecting on Crozet during the 1960's, Rev. Nathan Fox, a former pastor of Crozet Baptist Church, observed, "We are prone to look at the people who speak in public and those who have a more glamorous testimony. And yet there are many saints that we don't hear from too much."

When I was growing up in Crozet, Frank and Edwina Wyant lived in a house on Main Street that stood about where the Crozet Farmer's Market is held today. Mr. Wyant would set a small table at the end of his sidewalk and sell produce he grew in his backyard garden. I can still picture him there, wearing his old straw hat against the summer sun, serving up vegetables to the town.

Fred Brown has lived a few miles north of Crozet since the late 1950's. Searching for a better

The clubhouse for the Woman's Club of Crozet was built in 1928. Over the years it also served as the meeting place for other service groups, such as the Lion's Club and scouting organizations. Many social activities were held in its comfortable quarters. [Photo courtesy of the Woman's Club of Crozet.]

way to cultivate his garden, Fred chanced upon an old one-wheeled (by design) garden tractor. He spent many hours restoring it to like-new condition, and then used it to take care of his garden. But it wasn't until he displayed it at a steam-and-gas show that he realized the greatest joy of all—sharing his knowledge of these machines with others seeking a glimpse of a by-gone era. Fred's form of community outreach has extended to several counties around us.

The ever-increasing stream of cyclists passing by June Curry's house in Afton allows her all the opportunity she needs to exercise her compassion for others. By providing a cool drink of water, fresh-baked cookies, and a safe place to rest, June has touched the hearts of literally thousands of weary travelers—and she didn't have to leave home to do it. Cyclists from around the world attest to the kindness of this community because of one person doing just what they could to make someone else's journey a little easier.

5

Sugar Hollow Reservoir:
A Cool Drink of Water

By September 1946, several of the 14 concrete sections comprising the dam were taking shape. [Photo courtesy of Rivanna Water and Sewer Authority (RWSA).]

Nothing satisfies the thirst like a good, cool drink of water.

For the wary citizens of Charlottesville in the early 1920s, a very *un*-satisfying sight was the dwindling reserve of potable water adjacent to their new Lewis Mountain water filter plant. By the fall of 1923, a variety of groups and individuals were using the pulpit of Charlottesville's *Daily Progress* newspaper to trumpet the impending crisis:

"DON'T WASTE WATER! Waste now means ruin later… The situation is critical… Visit the reservoir and see how little is left for urgent need… Saving is our only salvation…"

Engineering firms evaluated a half dozen or more possible sources for additional water supply and unanimously pointed toward Moorman's River in western Albemarle County, with its Blue Ridge Mountains watershed stretching from Jarman's Gap to Brown's Gap. A decision was made to construct an intake near William James's ford in Sugar Hollow, near the confluence of the south and north forks of that mountain stream.

The initial dam built near James's Ford was only three feet in height. Its purpose was to divert a steady portion of the stream's flow through a hand-valve and into an 18-inch pipe where gravity funneled the water nearly 14 miles to the city's filter plant. By early 1925, the impound's daily average output of 2½ million gallons of water was providing a surplus to the growing town's water requirements.

The Moorman's River location actually had been eyed since the late-teens as a potential site for a large reservoir capable of meeting Charlottesville's water needs for many decades to come. Periodic seasonal droughts helped to maintain such a lofty idea in the backs of the planners' minds.

Sugar Hollow native William James (1866–1931) consulted with the project's earliest planners, and was employed as the initial on-site caretaker of the waterworks. He was succeeded at death by his son Charlie, who protected and maintained the Moorman's River facility for the next 42 years. At Charlie James' retirement, he, in turn, was succeeded by his grandson Billy James, who extended the family's faithful tradition of oversight of the Sugar Hollow Dam across six decades, until his own departure in 1979.

When the City of Charlottesville purchased the mountain acreage for their planned water impound, a number of families were still living in the mountainous watershed area. It was determined that their potential impact on water quality would be negligible. In 1926, the establishment of Shenandoah National Park was authorized by Congress. By 1928, land surveys had been made in preparation for acquisition of the Park lands, and all but a few of the nearby mountain

Flooding rains, spawned by Hurricane Isabel in September 2003, poured over the dam in Sugar Hollow and overwhelmed the Moorman's River downstream.

families had moved away.

Any acreage flooded by a potential future reservoir would be on city-owned lands, but the watershed itself would be inside The Park. In May 1928, the Director of the National Park Service met with local officials to assure them that park rangers and wardens would be diligent in protecting the Moorman's River water supply from fire and contamination.

Concerns fueled by international unrest and our nation's own economic depression restricted the monies necessary to expand the initial impound into the soon-to-be-needed mountain reservoir. However, in 1935, the idea was advanced further when Civilian Conservation Corps labor from Camp Albemarle in White Hall relocated the pioneer trail passing through Sugar Hollow and placed the new roadbed above the future dam.

In the fall of 1941, the City Commissioners appropriated money to clear trees, rocks and undergrowth from the area near the Moorman's River intake—

Sugar Hollow born-and-bred, Charlie James assumed the role of caretaker of Moorman's River Dam from his father in 1931. Self-described as "the Sheriff of Sugar Hollow," he maintained the reservoir's waterworks for 42 years. [Photo courtesy of Billy James.]

taking yet another step toward expanding their future water storage capacity. Within weeks, though, when the United States formally entered into World War II, all plans for expansion were placed quickly on indefinite hold. Not until victory was achieved did the work move forward again.

In April of 1946, Faulconer Construction Company began preparatory work at the site of the Moorman's River Dam. They established the on-site physical plant necessary to carry out the monumental task, and began excavation work for the dam's foundation.

Neither before nor since has this section of the Blue Ridge Mountains experienced such an

Construction work on Moorman's River Dam began in earnest in April 1946. This was the westward view, looking back upstream to the 1925 intake works. [Photo courtesy of RWSA.]

The original Moorman's River Intake alleviated Charlottesville's water concerns beginning in 1925. The shed in the foreground sheltered the hand-valve that controlled the water flow. [Photo courtesy of the McAllister collection]

operation. A gas pump and oil tank were set into place to fuel the machinery. Upstream, the Moormans' north fork was diverted into the south fork, allowing the placement of construction access roads. A 20-ton hoisting derrick with a boom radius of 115' was mounted; an electric power plant and air compressors were set up; a rock crushing and screening operation was built in place to serve the concrete mixing plant. A so-called "dinky railroad" was put into place—yes, a railroad in Sugar Hollow—to move the concrete into position to be hoisted and poured into the forms; a full-sized carpenter's shop for cutting lumber to construct the forms was built, as was a blacksmith shop and tool shed to maintain the machinery and fabricate whatever special apparatus might be needed in day-to-day operations. Offices were built for the contractors and engineers.

The dam's superstructure was designed to be nearly 500' long end-to-end, with retaining walls extending an additional 30' on each side. Its height was 67' from the bedrock base to the spillway lip.

Visitors have been attracted by Sugar Hollow's rugged landscape for generations. This group paused to contemplate the peaceful waters of the reservoir in 1949. [Photo courtesy of the Dunn-Bing collection]

It was poured in 14 sections, or blocks, and the rock blasted or removed from the area was reused in the concrete pours.

Atop the structure, steel gates were installed to adjust maximum water levels; this system was used until 1999 when they were replaced with an inflatable bladder.

The mountain facility, titled the Moorman's River Dam by its designers, has been known locally by various other names through the years, including: Charlottesville Reservoir, Sugar Hollow Dam, Moorman's River Intake and the Sugar Hollow Reservoir. It has been viewed from on high by many millions of tourists to Shenandoah National Park from the Skyline Drive's overlook at Milepost 92, situated 2,000 feet above the spillway's lip.

Faithful caretakers have often endured dangerous conditions to keep the dam safe and the water flowing properly, while appreciating one of this region's most beautiful work locations. Hurricane-bred floodwaters have tried to overwhelm the structure many times, but the diligence of the many laborers who saw to it that the designers' instructions were followed accurately has assured the structure's survival.

The major motion picture *Evan Almighty* featured a view of the reservoir with digitized effects, and a reliable source has hinted that another yet-to-be-released motion picture has used the reservoir's backdrop in a special scene.

Recreationalists have documented their visits to the Sugar Hollow area of western Albemarle County since the mid-1800s. With its National Park backdrop and cool, refreshing waters, this very special place will be part of the unique memories and lore of future generations.

6
Summer Rest

SUMMER REST, GREENWOOD, VA.

Summer Rest's main lodge was built in 1896. Additional cottages were later added to the grounds.

"Summertime," wrote Gershwin in his lullaby, "and the living is easy."

In earlier times, the affluent retreated from the stifling summer heat of the cities and the disease-prone low-country. From the mid-1850s, Virginia's western mountains and springs were the summer destination for many. Traveling via bateau, private carriage, public stagecoach, and, later, rail, these early vacationers fueled the infant industry of recreational travel and leisure: travel—simply for the sake of adventure; and leisure—simply because one could.

Families of the planters from Virginia's Tidewater region, joined along the way by Richmond's social elite, passed through central Virginia and the wind gaps in the mountains of western Albemarle County. Many were en route to luxury spas and resorts advertising a multitude of "entertainments" accompanied by spring waters whose natural elixirs proclaimed the powers of rejuvenation and healing.

Black Rock Springs, west of Sugar Hollow, just over the mountain into Augusta County, proclaimed as early as the 1830s to be "superior to all the spas of Europe." Its rustic location found special appeal with Shenandoah Valley residents as well as others east of the Blue Ridge.

More easily accessible but modest accommodations could be had along the way at the White Hall home of George Brown and his daughter, Mollie. Formerly a tavern and stagecoach stop, the Brown's early 19th-century-constructed home found good favor in 1907 with young sisters Grace and Eliza Heyl from Norfolk. Accompanied by their mother, they were sent to the mountains from their home in Norfolk's Ghent section to preserve their health during the hot, steamy months. Their daily leisure activities included the excitement of exchanging postcards with their father and other family members.

In 1894 Albemarle County's mountain resort Summer Rest greeted its first patrons even as a decline was being experienced by many of the region's 19th-century retreats. Quite unlike the business profile of the earlier elitist resorts, its "mission" was to provide relaxing, affordable summer accommodations to working-class women from the Richmond area.

"Summer Rest was built by the Episcopal Church as a place for working girls like secretaries to have a reasonable place they could come for some summer vacation," recalled the late C. Purcell McCue of Greenwood. "So they came up on the train. Somebody locally was employed who had an automobile to meet the train and get them over there and take them to different places."

In the early 1890s, Miss Grace Evelyn Arents, the noted philanthropist from Richmond, Virginia, became aware of the need of her town's single working ladies to have a place where they could spend a restful retreat away from the rigors of the busy city. And during those economically depressed days it was especially important that they could afford the costs associated with an extended stay. Miss Arent's devotion to the work of the Episcopal Diocese of Virginia and her des-

Hikers could enjoy this sweeping view of the Piedmont Valley from the C&O Railroad near Summer Rest.

The parlor at Summer Rest. On the occasional cool, damp day, guests were soothed by a fire in the parlor's fireplace.

Sheep grazed inside a field ringed by a split-rail fence adjacent to the front lawn of Summer Rest.

View from the front porch of Summer Rest, looking toward Humpback Mountain. *Next page:* **A corner of the library at Summer Rest, near Greenwood.**

ignated monetary gift led to that group's establishing the Summer Rest facilities in western Albemarle County near Greenwood Depot.

For decades, postcard messages attested to the success of Arent's vision and also to the care which Richmond's "working girls" received while they enjoyed their mountain retreat. In 1906 J.M.M. wrote to a friend in Petersburg: "A beautiful place & so restful. About 1½ miles from the station."—Another wrote in 1914: "This is a beautiful place and we like it fine. Took a long walk yesterday. Everything is grand. This is the hotel [referring to the postcard's view]. Write to us. Love to all, Lelah. Summer Rest, Greenwood, Va."—Written in 1910, "I am enjoying the fresh air and good water so much, expect to come home strong and fat. I am feeling better already. Florence"

During the pre-WWI heyday of the postcard craze, Summer Rest's postcard offerings also provided a handsome historical record of that area. Their numerous picture postcards highlighted various views of the Summer Rest façade and porches. These were accompanied by scenes of local fruit orchards, Humpback Mountain, the railroad tunnel entrances constructed by Claudius Crozet's workers, "the station for Summer Rest" and the hotel at Greenwood—each card preserving for posterity a glimpse back at a bygone era when convenient rail travel and comfortable, homey accommodations combined to meet the travel needs of many.

The property's guest register eventually recorded the inclusion of men and married couples. In 1940 they hosted Episcopal Archdeacon of the Blue Ridge Frederick W. Neve's "Conference of Mountain Workers. " A watermelon feast, games of horseshoes and camaraderie enjoyed on the hotel's covered porches and tree-shaded lawn made for a festive, relaxing occasion.

For guests, leisurely mornings were complemented with bird-songs from the trees and bushes dotting the spacious lawn. These gave way to hikes and pic-nics or an occasional trip into the 'burg of Charlottesville or

Waynesboro. Afternoons might include letter writing, reading a book chosen from the hotel's library, or a peaceful nap. Evening entertainments sometimes included inviting "eligible" guests from the neighborhood to participate in a cake walk or dance or to simply enjoy polite conversa-tion while a record played in the background. And always—always—delicious meals!

Advertising in 1946, fifty-two years after hosting its first guests, Summer Rest promoted itself thusly: "Situated in the Blue Ridge Mountains of Virginia. Quiet, Restful, Beautiful Scenery. All Modern Conveniences. Room and Board by Week. Single room. Two in room. Three or more in room. Cinder block cabins. Shower baths."

Summer Rest and its congenial staff played host to many weary city folk for three-quarters of a century. Only a few got more "rest" than they had bargained for, far away from the bright lights of the big city, as one succinctly wrote in a letter in 1917: "Believe me this place has its correct name. This is the only place I have ever been that I could rest. Nothing to do. Lots of love, Ruth"

Many, however, found the repose they came seeking, and returned year after year: "Don't you wish you were here! Go west my boy. Go west."—"I am waiting patiently for your letter. I hope you… will write me soon and tell me… all about your dear self."—"Wish you could be here with me. Having a grand time."

Today, near western Albemarle County's Newtown community, a road named Summer Rest Lane is situated alongside I-64. The final closing of Summer Rest around 1965, followed by the excavation and construction of the interstate in the late-1960s and early '70s, contributed to the removal of most of the old retreat's facilities.

Reflecting on his 1895 stay at George Brown's White Hall hotel/boarding establishment, the Rev. D.G.C. Butts penned these words: "Hospitality and good food and freedom from care ruled the household, and everybody felt at home." It is probably safe to say that the vast majority of the guests at old Summer Rest would have echoed those same words. Oh, that we could all pen a postcard home with a similar sentiment from our vacations today.

7

Morton's:
"An Old Kentucky Recipe"

It took 18 trucks and drivers to fulfill one frozen food order to a Pittsburgh wholesaler in the late 1950's. That was a lot of dinner rolls and mac'-and-cheese!

Older homes are often referenced by the original owner's name, i.e. the old Wayland place, Knobloch's Corner, or the Ballard house. Sometimes the names change to reflect a newer generation's associations. We identify with our own neighborhoods and sometimes are identified by the neighborhoods in which we live.

Similar parallels can be made to the places where we work. Just as in our home neighborhoods, we also nurture business friendships, calling on co-workers in times of need, and finding opportunities to celebrate together. We develop a unique identity at our workplaces and often are identified by the places where we work.

Crozet and much of western Albemarle County was defined economically by a thriving fruit industry beginning in the late 1800s. In the first decade of the 20th century, fruit production had exceeded immediate seasonal demands. William Carter, who was operating an ice plant alongside the railroad in downtown Crozet, began an expansion to his facility in 1912 to include a six-story cold storage plant. This new enterprise—known later as Herbert Cold Storage and Ice Company—allowed for the storage of apples that remained unsold at the end of picking time.

By 1929, a second cold storage plant was placed in operation a short distance east

CROZET FROZEN APPLES
SUGAR ADDED FIVE PLUS ONE
NET WEIGHT 30 POUNDS

SUGGESTED RECEIPT FOR USE IN PIES

Let apple slices completely defrost. Drain all the juice from the container. To this juice, add 1 lb. Sugar, 8 lbs. Water and 8 lbs. Corn Syrup. Bring this to a hard boil, add 1 lb. Corn Starch, Cinnamon, Nutmeg and salt to taste.

Pour this hot liquid over defrosted apple slices. Let stand until cool. Mixture is then ready for pies. *Do not fill pies with hot mix.*

PACKED BY
CROZET COLD STORAGE CORPORATION
CROZET, VIRGINIA

With the addition of a fruit peeling-and-slicing operation in the mid-1940's, the Crozet Cold Storage achieved a marketable product line.

of the C&O depot. Operated as the Crozet Cold Storage, apple storage space could be rented on a per barrel basis by smaller fruit growers. A.E. Rea, a well-known Crozet grocer, offered an additional service that included the cutting, wrapping and freezing of fresh meats. Grocers and individuals could rent storage lockers for meats, fruits and vegetables.

Several additions to the Morton Frozen Foods physical plant are evident in this 1959 photo that Les Gibson took from his front yard across the street. The Beitzel home, partially visible to the left, was later moved to make way for the plant's cafeteria.

The Crozet Cold Storage, in operation by 1929, was Crozet's second major fruit storage facility. Herbert's Cold Storage, adjacent to the C&O railroad depot and The Square, had already been in service for over ten years.

A peeling-and-slicing plant was added onto the Crozet Cold Storage in 1946, and Crozet Frozen Foods was born. Sliced, frozen apples and peaches were packaged and sold for uses such as pie fillings. During fruit season this operation required two shifts of workers to meet demand.

But as the fruit industry began to wane in the 1940's, the large, local, able-bodied workforce began to turn to nearby towns to find other employment. While small-scale subsistence farming still supported some residents, industries in Charlottesville and Waynesboro attracted people needing steady employment. With the arrival of Acme Visible Records in 1950, the fortunes of many local residents took a positive turn. Year-round inside work, fair wages and benefits packages began to redefine a people long identified as seasonal laborers.

Meanwhile, a business that would forever influence our Crozet community emerged from unassuming beginnings west of our Blue Ridge Mountains. In 1940, in an abandoned church building in Louisville, Kentucky, Harold Morton developed a chicken-and-noodle dish, which he sold in glass jars. Following World War II, Morton entered the fledgling frozen food industry with the Chicken Pot Pie, made from an "Old Kentucky Recipe". Acceptance and demand led him to create more products including beef and turkey pot pies and, later, fruit and other frozen dessert pies. With his business growth limited by the capacities of his Louisville plant, Morton began to search for a larger frozen food production facility. His search ended in Crozet.

When the Morton Packing Company purchased the Crozet Cold Storage building in 1953 (as well as another similar operation in Webster City, Iowa), Harold Morton's former basement operation took a major leap forward.

In 1955, Continental Baking Company purchased Morton's business and operated it as a separate division. With the driving force of this major corporate parent, the Morton Frozen Foods operation in Crozet experienced amazing growth and success. During the next ten years the former Crozet Cold Storage physical plant was expanded almost annually. There was hardly a town in the United States in which the Morton label was not familiar.

By 1965, Morton Frozen Foods was Albemarle County's largest employer with over 1,600 employees working three shifts around the clock. Its fleet of 35 tractor-trailers, one of the largest in the county, traveled more than five million miles annually!

The consistently high quality, prepared frozen foods turned out by skilled co-workers not only made the company profitable, but it also made it a tempting acquisition in the corporate world. In addition to Continental Baking Company, the former Morton Packing Company was operated at different times under the giant corporate umbrellas of International Telephone and Telegraph, Del Monte, R.J. Reynolds, and Nabisco. In 1986 it was acquired by ConAgra Frozen Foods who owned it until a corporate streamlining brought about the Crozet plant's closure in the fall of 2000.

Pauline Corbin was one of the employees who started work at Morton's on its first day of operations in Crozet. "We started at seventy-five cents an hour," she recalled, "and didn't get any raises until the Union came in." For the next 35 years, laboring in numerous departments on both sides of the road, she weathered the plant's consistent growth, including its advancements in automated production. Summing up her varied work experiences recently, she concluded, "We had a lot of fun. It was really nice down there."

Gone now is the railroad spur that crossed Rt. 240 to transport raw materials to the freezer/

With appealing advertisements in major magazines and on television, Morton 'prepared frozen foods' achieved popularity throughout the United States.

Crozet, Virginia marketed its advantages in the 1933 Shenandoah National Park visitor's guide. Identifying itself as 'Home of the famous Albemarle Pippins', it also noted that the Crozet Cold Storage was 'Modern in every detail.'

warehouse across the street. Gone is the row of employees sitting on the rock wall in front of the old plant, catching up on news from one another while waiting for their rides at quitting time. Gone, too, is the seemingly endless line of traffic threading its way through Crozet following workshift changes. Gone are the crowds hoping to get best pickings at the Thrift Store on Saturday mornings, the occasional blast of a tractor-trailer horn, and the sweet smells that wafted across the road when honey buns were being prepared.

Once described as a small city that never slept, the Morton/Del Monte/ConAgra manufacturing facility was ably served by a family of co-workers who exemplified loyalty and steadfastness to their company and to one another. The values of the several thousands of employees who labored there across five decades continue to influence our local community, as well as many communities in the surrounding counties.

It was 80 years ago this year that construction began on a "new" cold storage facility in Crozet. Today, new tenants there perform vastly different tasks than those from that earlier era. May the legacies they leave reflect the excellent qualities of those workers who have gone before them.

An early photo of Blackwell men and boys. Back row, L–R: Ellis Blackwell, Robert Blackwell. Front row, L–R: James L. "Bose" Blackwell, Dave Blackwell, Earnest Blackwell, Jim Henry Blackwell. [Photo courtesy of Larry Lamb.]

8

Blackwell's Hollow—
From the Past to the Future

St. John the Evangelist Chapel stands in the foreground of this 1916 photo. The chapel was destroyed by fire in 1932, along with a school building and the mission worker's house. The structure in the background, serving as a clothing bureau, was spared.

It is a gift that will keep on giving.

In 2004, Robert Byrom of Blackwell's Hollow in northwest Albemarle County, generously donated 600 acres of his family's farm to Albemarle County for use as a recreational forest preserve. Given in honor of his wife, Patricia Byrom, this newest and largest recreational area in Albemarle County will be named the Patricia Ann Byrom Forest Preserve Park. A network of roads and trails on the property—which borders Shenandoah National Park—is envisioned by the county's Parks and Recreation Department to provide recreational opportunities such as hiking and mountain biking.

Blackwell's Hollow is a beautifully rugged valley, bordered on its west side by the Loft Mountain area which includes the Little Flat and Big Flat Mountains, and on the east side by the

Blackwell's Hollow Store. Following her husband's death in 1948, Lucy Ruebush Walton had this log structure built across the road from her home in Blackwell's Hollow and operated it as a full-service grocery store, complete with gasoline pump.

Fox Mountain area which includes the High Top, Martin and Gibson Mountains.

Visitors to this natural area will not only enjoy the benefits of the Byrom family's 40 years of faithful stewardship of this unspoiled mountain land, but they will also have access to a portion of the ancestral lands originally occupied by the Colonial-era family who lent their name to the Blackwell's Hollow section of the county.

William Blackwell purchased his first parcel of land in Albemarle County in 1767. After his death in 1775, his son and subsequent generations of ancestors continued to acquire land through purchases and grants that eventually totaled over 2,000 acres.

Having been peopled for well-over two hundred years, the Blackwell's Hollow area has a rich cultural history. Like the storied Brown family of Brown's Cove, the Blackwell family prospered by their industriousness and contributed to their local economy. In addition to orchards and other agricultural pursuits, the Hollow was home to at least two licensed distilleries, a mill, and a tan yard.

The late Albemarle County historian Vera V. Via recounted the seriousness with which the early citizens of Blackwell's Hollow engaged in the politics, describing the area as "a political no man's land." In the mid-1800's, the voters of Blackwell's Hollow petitioned the Virginia General Assembly and a voting precinct was established at Blackwell's Tan Yard. Polling Day brought a great migration down from the mountains and tempers flared as opposing views were aired. Fist fights, rock throwing and gun play occurred. The voters of Blackwell Precinct took their politics passionately!

The spiritual needs of the people living in the remote hollows and heights of the Blue Ridge Mountains were addressed by the Reverend Frederick William Neve who was called to Ivy, Virginia, from his home in England in 1888. Because of his passion for and work among the people of the mountains, Reverend Neve was eventually appointed Archdeacon of the Blue Ridge by the Episcopal Church. Raising funds and securing faithful administrators such as Reverend George P. Mayo and Reverend W. Roy Mason, Neve's vision led to the establishment of schools and churches at scores of locations in the mountains of central Virginia.

In Blackwell's Hollow, a school, chapel, mission worker's home, and clothing bureau were established. Mission work was carried on in these buildings at St. John the Evangelist Chapel between 1905 and 1932. Shortly before Easter in 1932, a disastrous fire destroyed all of the buildings at the Blackwell's Hollow mission location except the one housing the clothing bureau.

Known for his determination in the face of difficult circumstances, Archdeacon Neve quickly arranged for a replacement. Since his very first rural mission, St. John the Baptist Episcopal Church (built with his own funds in 1890 near Ivy), had been replaced with a fieldstone structure in 1930, Neve had this original frame church dismantled and moved to Blackwell's Hollow. It was reassembled on a hillside about a mile from the former mission site. A new stone mission worker's house was also built at the new site.

In May, 1933, Neve's newsletter, *Our Mountain Work*, reported on the Day of Consecration for the newly rebuilt church: "On the 'Great Day in the Morning' a path from the skies was found by the falling rain. This, the so eagerly awaited morning, was dark. But from Richmond, from Tappahanock, from Fleeton, from Orange, from way up in Rappahannock County, from Pine Grove, from Ingham, from Yancey and Lynnwood, from Ivy and Charlottesville, and from every hollow and hill-side about

At home in Blackwell's Hollow, Earnest Blackwell (1868–1942) had just finished combing his favorite horse. [Photo courtesy of Larry Lamb.]

Lucy Ruebush Walton (1885–1959) was the wife of James Thomas Walton. In addition to bearing 12 children and managing her household well, she also operated the Blackwell's Hollow Store and used her profits to buy additional properties. [Photo courtesy of Pauline Walton Corbin.]

Blackwell's came Bishops, and Clergy and Lay people until the church was filled to over-flowing and some stayed outside. The rain fell steadily. The clouds lay softly on the surrounding peaks. It was a perfectly lovely rainy day!"

The "new" St. John the Evangelist Church in Blackwell's Hollow continued to serve its community from 1932 until 1948. It later served as a Boy's Home.

A rugged valley with a rugged people fit to meet the challenges presented to them—that has been one face of the history of Blackwell's Hollow. Succeeding years have brought a gentler face to the Hollow. Many descendants of the original Blackwell family still call the Hollow home. Other families with deep roots in Blackwell's Hollow continue to reside there as well, including Frazier, Garrison, Gibson, Morris, Shifflett, Via, and Walton descendants.

To ride north from Crozet still gives today's traveler many glimpses back to Albemarle County's rural past. Orchards of apples and peaches decorate the countryside with their fragrant blooms in the springtime, and with the busyness of harvest time. Well–kept gardens, vineyards and farm lands depict the traditional rhythms of the seasons. Farmers still cut and bale hay, harvest cornfields and tend to cattle and horses. Rustic barns and log structures remind us of earlier days. Apple butter boilings are still held in autumn, with community members pitching in to peel the apples and help stir the kettles. Churches host community hymn–sings and welcome members and visitors for regular Sunday services and revivals. Church yards fill with cars for annual homecomings with dinner–on–the–grounds.

The anticipated opening of the Patricia Ann Byrom Forest Preserve Park will encourage many other county residents to visit this unique section of Albemarle County and to experience for themselves the natural beauty that has been enjoyed by others for so many years.

The southern end of Blackwell's Hollow Road begins at the bridge over the Doyle's River, 6.5 miles north of White Hall on Brown's Gap Turnpike. The entrance to Patricia Ann Byrom Forest Preserve Park will be approximately 1.9 miles north of this intersection.

9
Civilian Conservation Corps
75th Anniversary, 1933 – 2008

Civilian Conservation Corps Camp Albemarle, 1933–1942, was located at White Hall, northwest of the intersection of present-day Brown's Gap Turnpike and Sugar Hollow Road. During WWII it was converted into an internment camp for German prisoners-of-war. [Photo courtesy of NACCCA archives.]

The roaring that characterized the 1920s in America subsided to a whimper by the early '30s. Society's fortunate who had lived with lavish excess simply withdrew into more moderate patterns. But for the many who perpetually lived on the margin, especially those in urban areas, economic hard times meant being without. The double-whammy of nationwide climatic extremes soon brought the realities of true hard times to the rural population as well. Millions wondered how much more they could take.

Walter McDowell (1914 – 2007) was a teenager living in tidewater Virginia during the early 1930s. The economic downturn had severely curtailed his father's work as a house carpenter. "There wasn't any work to be done," the younger McDowell recalled. "Kids just roaming the streets. You couldn't find a job anywhere. It was right in the Depression. You couldn't even have bought a job then—if you had had any money."

The son of a waterman from Kinsale, Virginia, J. Harvey Bailey Jr. (1909 – 2003) was a 1931 graduate of V.P.I. with a degree in civil engineering. His new academic credentials, however, did not shield him from the uncertainties of the times. When project funding was reduced for the mapping work he was doing for the Coast and Geodetic Survey, Bailey resorted to occasional survey work and short term teaching stints. One such assignment was a mathematics class at the remote Blue Ridge Industrial School near the Greene and Albemarle County border.

Bailey stated, "President Hoover did not return to the White House in 1932. Franklin D. Roosevelt was his successor. The campaign was run on the ability of which candidate could propose and manage a plan which would bring the country to an economy that would furnish a fair

African-American enrollees from CCC Camp Gallion in Green Bay, Virginia, were reassigned to Camp Albemarle in June, 1941. They were tasked in 1941–'42 with finishing the Lake Albemarle dam. [Photo courtesy of J. Harvey and Margaret Bailey.]

living and assist the individual to support a family and to seek employment where it was offered. The problem before the Federal government stretched across the country. Employment had to be found and distributed country-wide."

The first 100 days following Roosevelt's inauguration are legendary. His "New Deal" programs were aimed at providing immediate economic relief to the masses and instilling hope for the future. On March 21, 1933, seventeen days after his inauguration, Roosevelt called on Congress to adopt his plan for Unemployment Relief:

"I propose to create a civilian conservation corps to be used in simple work, not interfering with normal employment, and confining itself to forestry, the prevention of soil erosion, flood control and similar projects …The overwhelming majority of unemployed Americans, who are now walking the streets and receiving private or public relief, would infinitely prefer to work. We can take a vast army of these unemployed out into healthful surroundings. We can eliminate to some extent at least the threat that enforced idleness brings to spiritual and moral stability."

The Emergency Conservation Work Act was signed into law on March 31, 1933, creating the Civilian Conservation Corps program. Just 17 days later, the first C.C.C. camp in the United States—appropriately named Camp Roosevelt—was established near Luray, Virginia. By early July, over 300,000 young men and their leaders were enrolled in over 1,400 camps in every state of the Union.

The pathway into the CCCs led first to "conditioning camp" for most of the new enrollees. It was there that Portsmouth teenager Walter McDowell was assigned to an office group processing the stream of fellow recruits. "They sent us to Fort Monroe [Virginia] Army Training Camp. I stayed there about a month. The first group that I was with went up on the Skyline Drive right close to the north end of it. I stayed in Monroe and we shipped 'em out by train and by truck. When they got 'em all out they put us on a train and sent us up to Crozet."

It was early Sunday morning, June 11, 1933, when 176 sleepy-tired young men detrained at the C&O Depot in Crozet. They had been assigned to C.C.C. Company 338, Camp Albemarle.

"Trucks met us there and we unloaded our clothes and whatever we had off the train into the truck and they carried us up there and put us on that vacant field at White Hall," recalled McDowell. "Peach orchard on one side of it. Moorman's River right down below us. When they dumped us out there the only bath we had was the river. Threw some tents out with us and said 'ya'll put 'em up if you want to sleep inside.' So we were learning right from the start. Dumped the cooking stuff out and they cooked outdoors until we built a mess hall. We were right out in the open. Yeah, a bunch of kids turned loose there with three Army officers. They helped us out with how to set up tents and stuff like that. We didn't know a thing about it! On the job training."

Eight days later the temporary tent camp was in order and the first work crews were turned over to the "Using Service." For the next month, a lack of available trucks required the boys to walk six to eight miles a day to and from their initial assignments of establishing fire trails in the nearby mountains. By July the mess hall was under roof, and in September the shower house was completed. Winter-like conditions arrived in October and the completion of the permanent barracks in November was a celebrated event. As Walter McDowell reminisced, "That was the good life then. You were getting three meals a day. Place to sleep. Lot of them didn't have a place to sleep if they went back home. I really enjoyed it. I had a good time there."

Administered by the U.S. Army and assigned work by the Virginia Forest Service, Camp

The Camp Exchange, or PX, offered snacks, tobacco and sundries for sale to enrollees. The store's profits were reinvested in the recreation hall's amenities and the leisure activities in the camp. [Photo courtesy of Truman and Elva Huckstep.]

Camp Albemarle's CCC enrollees slept in five barracks measuring 20' X 110' each. All of the camp's facilities were maintained with a military-style neatness. [Photo courtesy of Truman and Elva Huckstep.]

Albemarle operated for nine years—the duration of the CCC program. Several thousand young men benefited from the training and guidance they received in the rolling Blue Ridge foothills of western Albemarle County.

CCC camps were segregated by race and Camp P60–VA was established as an all-white camp. In June, 1941, with much attrition in the camp due to an improving economy and the build-up of the nation's military machine, men from African-American Company 1390, Camp Gallion, located in Green Bay, Virginia, were transferred to White Hall. Camp Albemarle was then assigned the new designation of "S60–VA", denoting the camp's work focus change from working on predominantly private or "P" lands to state-owned or "S" lands. The reassigned enrollees from Camp Gallion worked to complete construction of the Lake Albemarle dam project that was begun in 1938.

J. Harvey Bailey was employed by the Forest Service in 1936 to be the engineer for CCC Camp Albemarle. He retained that position until the program closed in 1942. In a letter to this writer, Bailey reflected on the work of the Moorman's River/White Hall camp: "Camp P-60, sometimes called Moorman's River, sometimes White Hall, was one of the several who did work especially on suppression of forest fire. It built truck trails; improved secondary public roads; bridges (to expedite access to isolated peaks and valleys); built telephone lines to connect fire marshals; erected and manned fire lookout towers. The machine shop and equipment brought on additional work from camps over the state. After an equipment plant was built at Salem for repairs and storage, Camp P60 hauled equipment to it. Its personnel built a pile driver to construct a rather lengthy body of water in eastern Virginia; prepared a topo-map of about 300 acres of the

University of Virginia; built an impound for a recreational area—Lake Albemarle—to be used by the state. Nor should we forget the feeding of birds during the harsh winters."

President Roosevelt's CCC boys lived out their unofficial motto: "WE CAN TAKE IT!" Over three million young men were enrolled in the corps during its nine-year run. Today, 75 years hence, our society continues to enjoy the fruits of their labors. A tremendous debt of gratitude is still owed to the organizers and laborers in that remarkable chapter of our nation's history.

J. Harvey Bailey Jr. holds a 1938 CCC Camp Albemarle roster photo. Its parquetry frame was made in the camp's cabinet shop. Bailey was the camp's principal engineer and his six years of service there was among the longest of any on the technical staff.

The group of CCC enrollees who arrived at Camp Albemarle in June, 1933, lived in army tents for five months while they constructed more permanent facilities. [Photo courtesy of Eldon and Mary Morris.]

10

Free Union, Virginia

Maupin Brothers (with adjacent gasoline station) was at least the third store on this corner in downtown Free Union. Their business—which at one time also housed the Free Union P.O.—operated there from 1928 until 1961 when it was moved into another nearby building. [Courtesy Dunn-Bing family archives.]

Why has Free Union, Virginia, so captured the attention of historians and writers through the years? Perhaps because this rural crossroads town embodies certain gentleness; the architecture along its principal travel routes harkens to the pleasant memories of an earlier time.

Most of the rolling acres in the area had already been claimed when, in the mid-eighteenth century, redrawing county lines put the Free Union area within the new county of Albemarle instead of Louisa. The culture of tobacco planters and their enslaved workforce set the tone in those early years. By Revolutionary times, travelers passing through this region on the Buck Mountain Road could find respite at Michie's Ordinary two miles east of Free Union. There, a meal and ardent spirits could be had and a bed might be procured for the overnight.

In early days, the Buck Mountain Road was a string of roads that stretched from Rockfish Gap, meandered along the eastern base of the Blue Ridge Mountains, passed through Earlysville and ended near Stony Point on the Barboursville road; it became this countryside's defining thoroughfare. The Mechum's and Moorman's Rivers conjoin near Free Union and form the South Fork Rivanna River that once carried the commercial hopes of the surrounding region southeastward toward the James River at Columbia.

Free Union Baptist Church was established in 1833, and, in 1837, the congregation partnered with Episcopal, Methodist and Presbyterian groups to acquire land with a house for worship, agreeing to share the "meeting house" for their respective religious services. The Baptists eventually became sole possessors of the church building as the other three denominations established individual church sites. The Church of the Brethren started a preaching point in Free Union in 1885.

Free Union was originally known as Nicksville, being identified by the name of the African-American blacksmith who had established his workshop near the village's eventual commercial center. When the growing population needed a post office in 1847, they adopted the name of the local church to avoid confusion with another similarly-named county post office.

Vera Viola Via (1914–1964), eminent Albemarle County historian and much-beloved daughter of Free Union, recorded the oral tradition that, following the Civil War, the Free Union meeting house was used as a school for the elementary education of African-American children. James Ferguson, a surveyor by occupation, taught eleven students at what was perhaps the first school of its sort in Albemarle County.

Gradual improvements in roads and bridges encouraged the earliest growth patterns. Teamsters hauled the colonial commodities of tobacco and grains to commercial markets. Blacksmiths and wheelwrights quickly found their services needed, as did cabinet and furniture makers, as the local planters prospered. Water-

Free Union boasted an accredited high school in its earlier days. Following the establishment of Meriwether Lewis High School in Ivy, Virginia, the Free Union school housed elementary grades until further school consolidations brought its closing. [Courtesy Dunn-Bing family archives.]

One of Free Union's full-service stores was operated by E. J. T. Maupin. Services on his corner included gasoline sales and vehicle repairs.

A community park was once located in Free Union near the intersection of Buck Mountain and Free Union Roads. Amenities included seating and an outdoor fireplace—a delightful place to relax on an autumn day in 1940. [Courtesy Dunn-Bing family archives.]

powered mills eventually gave way to gasoline-fueled engines that ground the grains for local bread, animal feed, and commercial export.

General mercantiles appeared, and competition among them provided choice and convenience, contributing to and further inducing growth in and around Free Union. This pattern remained intact throughout rural America until after World War Two. Then, easier travel combined with greater urban labor needs began to pull workers from the countrysides. By the early 1950's industrial opportunities in Charlottesville, Earlysville and Crozet changed forever the face and pace of rural life and greatly impacted the commercial centers in small villages like Free Union.

In 1941 Free Union was honored by its selection as the location of the first county-sponsored 4–H youth camp in the state. 4–H *Camp Albemarle* (not to be confused with the former Civilian Conservation Corps camp of the same name located in White Hall) was sponsored by the Albemarle County Board of Supervisors. Funding and labor were provided by the depression-era relief program Work Projects Administration, along with a donation from the Albemarle Terracing Association, a group that encouraged soil erosion control and soil conservation. The rustic campground and lodge were built in a hollow alongside the Moorman's River. Although a number of upgrades have been made to the facility over the years, 67 years of happy campers coupled with hit-and-run vandalism have elevated the need for more regular maintenance and on-premises security. "The Campaign for Camp Albemarle" has been established to raise funds to meet these immediate needs and position the camp for many more years of service to youth.

Free Union native Sarah T. Dunn, along with her sister and fellow school teacher Isabelle Dunn Bing, maintained a keen interest in the early families of the Free Union area. The sisters'

Mt. Amos Baptist Church on the Free Union Road, c.1940s. African-American parishioners established separate houses of worship soon after the Civil War. [Courtesy Dunn-Bing family archives.]

shared hobbies also included the documentation of many of the older buildings around Free Union. (Several of the scenes accompanying this article were photographed by these community-minded women).

Among the items kept by Sarah Dunn was this poem:

What Is A Good Community?
Is it people working together regardless of any strife or weather?
Is it homes where privacy is assured and families' happiness can be secured?
Is it schools where children grow and democracy they learn to know?
Is it factories working night and day to speed production on its way?
Is it parks that are places of beauty and rest with children's playgrounds of the best?
Is it highways leading in and out to carry people and products about?
Is it different churches where you pray and serve your God in your own way?
Is it government that listens to you and does what the majority wants it to?
Is it a place where music and art flourish and the minds of men ever shall it nourish?
Is it housing of the best for all and there are no slums large or small?
It is all these things put together which will make a community go on forever.

Sarah and Belle read their own hopes for their community in the lines of this poem. As communities throughout the region prepare for inevitable change, the current stewards of Free Union strive—as did their predecessors—to maintain the gentle demeanor of their fair village.

11

The Glory Days of 250 West

The Tidbit Restaurant on 250 West was a popular gathering place for locals as well as travelers.

U.S. highway Rt. 250, west of Charlottesville—a.k.a. "250 West" to residents of western Albemarle County—has seen only minor changes to its routing since it first appeared on road maps around 1935. The most significant change to its path took place during the early 1940's when it was rerouted to bypass downtown Crozet. Another notable change created an easier road grade from the foot of the mountain near Brooksville to a junction just below the Blue Ridge Terrace. This improvement bypassed the quaint but treacherous switchbacks on the mountainside near the village of Afton.

America's love affair with the automobile—and road trips—blossomed following the sacrificial rationing of gasoline and tires necessitated by World War II. Service stations, restaurants and motels sprang up all across America, each one advertising to the ever-increasing stream of travelers driving by their roadside stands. A colorful assemblage of highway attractions, catering to the traveling public, prospered from the late-1940's well into the 1960's before a nationwide grid of sterile Interstate highways forever changed the face of roadside America.

Skipper's Restaurant, east of Ivy, was easily identified by this rooster on its neon road sign.

On 250 West, just 1½ miles east of Ivy, the motorist traveling after dark would have encountered a brightly colored neon rooster sporting a golf bag on his back, perched atop a sign for Skipper's Restaurant. The red and yellow duffer swung a broken golf club wildly at the surrounding tall, green neon grass. This critter was the logo for the restaurant chain *Chicken in the Rough.* The national franchise billed its signature menu item as "The World's Most Famous Chicken Dish: ½ Chicken Fried To A Golden Brown – Served Unjointed – Without Silverware." A motel was later built on the hillside behind Skipper's.

Just west of Ivy was the Siesta Motor Court with its colorful sign depicting a sombrero—wearing traveler sitting asleep at the base of a cactus. This motor court's original design featured garages with overhead doors for car security adjacent to each room. A large lawn in front of the rooms was outfitted with chairs and

The nicely appointed dining room at Blue Ridge Terrace on Afton Mountain enjoyed an early reputation for its Brunswick Stew.

Photographer Mac Sandridge captured this 1950's view of the Siesta Motor Court in Ivy.

umbrellas. The garages were later remodeled into additional guest rooms, and a restaurant was built next door.

Two miles west of the Siesta was Sunset Lodge. Situated along its driveway in a sweeping arc were individual "tourist cottages". The centerpiece of the property was its restaurant. An advertising postcard from the lodge, mailed in 1951 to "Dad" in New York, stated, "We are thru the Sky Line and I am pretty tired. This costs me $5.00 but worth it as I have to sleep. None last night."

Carl Morris's Oasis Restaurant at the Mechum's River junction of 250 West and Rt. 240 welcomed travelers with a full service menu: a full breakfast could be had for 75-cents; 25-cent burgers or a tempting 40-cent BLT were among the lunch options. At $2.75, the T-bone steak topped the dinner menu. Many can still recall when Harrison ("Pop") and Ethel Sandridge ran their popular eatery at this same location.

The E & S Motel, later renamed Greenwood Motel, was two miles west of Mechum's River. It billed itself as a "Gateway to the Skyline Drive." In the style of that day, it also included a restaurant.

Everyone likes choices and 7/10 of a mile farther west it probably got even harder for a family to make the decision on where to stop. By the time a driver arrived at Clover Lawn and The Tidbit he had encountered in the past 7 ½ miles: five (5) motels; six (6) restaurants; and four (4) service stations.

Walter and Ruby Radford's Clover Lawn Motel had guest cottages set a comfortable distance back from the road. Their snack bar, gift shop, and Mr. Radford's Esso gas station stood alongside the highway. Later, Clover Lawn Baskets occupied the former snack bar/gift shop.

On the opposite side of the highway, operating 24/7, was George Durham's popular Tidbit

Motel and Restaurant. Dining patrons had the option of curb service or eating in. The motorist's options were soon expanded to include a lighted, canopy covered, drive–up patio where they could order from and eat in their automobiles. The modern Tidbit Motel offered its guests the additional amenities of a swimming pool, a three-acre lake and a picnic area.

Preparing to depart in the morning, motel guests at the Tidbit Motel often found a card placed on their windshield by Buddy's Amoco Service, located right next door to the Tidbit. It read, "Good Morning! (Y'all). It has been our pleasure to Clean Your Windshield and we would welcome the opportunity to check your oil, water and battery before you continue your trip." This offer was made in a day and time when courtesies such as these were standard at "service" stations across the land.

Three additional opportunities for gasoline and two more food grills were encountered in the next 2 ½ miles before 250 West passed through the village of Yancey Mills. There, The Sign of the Green Teapot offered rooms and light meal fare in a wonderful old building that had served as a stagecoach tavern in the 18th century. Former Crozet residents Howard and Margaret Squire fondly recalled spending their honeymoon there. The menu for "Afternoon Tea" offered various breads, pastries and beverages. Tea, coffee, and cocoa were available at 25-cents a pot or 10-cents the cup.

Nearby and sitting quite literally at the edge of the road was The Dutch Gardens in Virginia. With its name sharing the theme of the neighboring Holland Floral Gardens, The Dutch Gardens featured a full–service restaurant bedecked with striped window awnings. A sign atop the restaurant also advertised their cottages—featuring "hot and cold running water".

Six miles west of Yancey Mills, 250 West began its noticeable ascent toward Rockfish Gap.

Sunset Lodge sat on a knoll above the highway, midway between Mechum's River and Ivy.

The Dutch Gardens, at Yancey Mills, was already providing meals and lodging to travelers in the 1930s.

The Tuckahoe Motel's neon-lit sign was encountered a short ways up the mountain, advertising the availability of air-conditioned rooms. Guests could also relax in the swimming pool or watch "Free TV".

Blue Ridge Terrace Hotel was the last stop for lodging before cresting the Blue Ridge at the junction of Skyline Drive and the Blue Ridge Parkway. Blue Ridge Terrace's 2,000-ft. elevation (or 1,800-ft., depending on the advertising) enhanced its popularity with the traveling public, affording its guests an unparalleled view across picturesque Rockfish Valley. Meals were available in the dining room throughout the day. Among the specialty menu items were Brunswick Stew, Waffle & Honey Dinners, and Ham Dinners featuring "Genuine Old Virginia Hickory Cured Ham, cured by 'Uncle Dan' the ham man, on his farm at Doylesville, Va.… cured by an old Colonial recipe and smoked with green hickory wood—brown as a berry and sweet as a nut." Rooms were available either in the hotel or across the highway in their hillside cottages.

It's bittersweet to recall the way we were, sometimes. If we think of this trip beginning one day back in the 1940s at Skipper's Chicken in the Rough, then it ended in December of '73 atop Afton Mountain. That was when I-64 was opened between Afton Mountain and Crozet, making an unbroken connection between I-95 at Richmond and I-81 at Staunton.

As automobile travel became more convenient than trains, most of the passenger rail depots closed. Many of the communities centered around the old depots disappeared, too. When Interstate highways became more convenient than local routes, many former service providers found themselves too far from the new interchanges to survive. A few were able to adapt to the lower traffic volume and found nurture from their local communities.

We were once satisfied with local conveniences and entertainments, but easier, faster avenues of transportation lured us farther and farther from home. After we settled back in we realized—too late—that the old familiar home place had irreversibly changed while we were away.

12

The Crozet Square

Storefronts on The Square in Crozet around 1914. L–R: J. M. Ellison's Store, Ballard & Rea, Crozet Hardware, Crozet Pharmacy. Upstairs over the pharmacy was Crozet Hotel.

The traditional heart of a town is its public square.

Some town squares are decorated with a statue, fountain or gardens, while others are more plainly appointed. But they all serve as a ready reference point where one can meet with acquaintances or just relax and take the pulse of the community.

The Miller Manual Labor School building project in the mid-1870s requested and received a whistle stop west of Mechum's River in western Albemarle County where building supplies could be conveniently off-loaded. A macadamized road of packed crushed stone led from the new depot to the school's construction site.

The rolling farm lands immediately surrounding that early whistle stop were un-noteworthy save for several groves of stately oaks. In the near distance could be seen the farm estate houses of the Ballard, Wayland and White families. Three-Notched Road, connecting the Shenandoah Valley with the State's capital at Richmond, traversed the area.

A dozen or more principal farmers and their extended families were well-established in the immediate area. Local enclaves of farm laborers and sharecroppers mingled with the influx of per-

A member of the Crozet High School Class of 1940, Clyde Sandridge worked the soda fountain at Crozet Drug and provided the pleasant service that business was known for. [Photo courtesy of Ruby Starke Sandridge.]

sons arriving by train to do business with and provide services for the new Miller School. Traveling businessmen soon took notice that many of their services and products had another customer base forming in the little railroad town.

By 1881, several entrepreneurs were already having their Crozet business relationships promoted through the Chesapeake & Ohio Railway's directory: Ben Woodson and his son William with blacksmith services; M. W. Wallace had a boarding-house; John W. Lyons was butchering meats; James M. Ellison, T. E. Powers and his brother, and M. W. Wallace ran competing mercantiles; W. H. Pannell and B. E. Smith had grist and lumber mills in operation; John Dollins and Robertson & Wallace provided nursery stock; and Lucian Hall had mounted his physician's shingle.

During the 1880s and '90s the village became more solidly established with enlarged freight facilities and the addition of a passenger depot. Passenger trains arrived mid-morning and late afternoon. The daily mail train came just before noon. Methodist and Episcopal churches, a hotel, livery and rental housing were serving the growing community.

Augusta County businessman James M. Ellison added to his portfolio a hotel within an easy stroll of the depot. The Liberty Hotel catered to the rail traveler visiting Miller School. It was also

Crozet Pharmacy, from 1904 until 1909, was attached to the west side of J. M. Ellison's Store, facing north toward the C&O Depot. L–R: Ellis Harris, Wiley Hughes astride the beast, John Moomaw (proprietor of the pharmacy), W. F. Carter Jr., unidentified dog wearing Carter's hat, and Russell Bargamin. [Photo courtesy of Mac Sandridge.]

discovered by vacationers from Richmond and points east and was affectionately referred to by one guest as "Ellison's old homestead."

When the founders of Crozet visualized their village's layout, they resisted the manner of some railroad towns that placed their commercial buildings just a wagon's length away from the clamor and dust of the passing trains. Instead, Crozet's visionaries stepped-off a public square which gave the merchants conve-

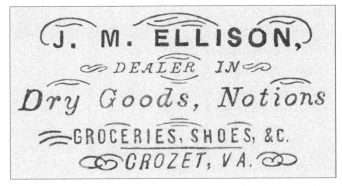

An 1880s advertising imprint from one of Crozet's earliest merchants, James Ellison.

nient access to the freight depot, while allowing their patrons a spacious lot to park their conveyances while they took care of business a more comfortable distance away.

During the first decade of the 20th-century, the Crozet Square was built out similarly to the way it appears today. The eastern-most of the businesses facing the C&O Depot was Ellison's General Store with apartments upstairs and an attached feed store. Sharing a wall with Ellison was John Moomaw's Crozet Pharmacy. Access to these businesses was made more convenient by a raised wooden walkway at their front entrances.

Stepping off the plank sidewalk, one crossed an alleyway to another feed storage building. This simple structure was redecorated in 1907 by Miss Dorothy Earp, and for a few years Crozet's

It was a busy day on The Square in 1953. This view looks past the former Ballard store building toward the S&S Food Center. A man and his best friend step past The Square's community Christmas tree. [Photo courtesy of the Woman's Club of Crozet.]

first lending library was housed there.

A stately, two-story red brick building anchored the corner of The Square adjacent to Miller School Avenue/Main Street by 1909, and was soon fully occupied with businesses. The Crozet Pharmacy relocated to this building with its front entrance angled toward the street. M. P. Sadler's Crozet Hardware Company was next door in the same building. Upstairs over the drug store and hardware was the Crozet Hotel, administered by Ellis Harris who was also Crozet's postmaster. Around back, in the same building, Jack Phillips barbered, repaired shoes and ran a print shop.

Filling in the gap between the old and new pharmacy locations, where the politely-appointed little library had stood, an imposing cement-block building was constructed. William Ballard partnered there with A. E. Rea to operate The Square's largest store, Ballard & Rea. Its commodious second floor was known as Ballard's Hall, and

The Freezer Fresh Ice Cream sign became a local trademark for George Pollock's Crozet Variety Store. For a penny, patrons could learn their weight and fortune on the way into the store. The entrance to Dan Bishop's shoe repair business was through the next door up the sidewalk. [Photo by Mac Sandridge.]

many community meetings and functions took place there. A contiguous cement sidewalk fronted this building and the hardware-hotel-pharmacy building next door.

In the 1940s, Ellison's old wood-framed store was razed and replaced with a cinder block building that housed the S&S Food Center. Like all of the grocery stores in Crozet at that time, the S&S took phone-in orders and made home-deliveries. Driving the grocery delivery trucks for the various stores was interesting work that suited many high school fellows. Sandridge's A&H/Western Auto expanded the building and offered a generous selection of furniture, televisions and appliances. A portion of their showroom was walled-off to establish a short-order grill operated at various times by Violet Collier & Lillian Vess, Pop & Ethel Sandridge, and, most notably, by Ollie & Dot Hutchinson as the Crozet Snack Corner.

As the decades passed, The Square did a good job of holding its own against growing competition around the village. The Crozet Pharmacy/Drug Store remained on the corner for many decades. The Crozet Hardware stayed on one side of The Square or the other, with only a change of owners. The hotels faded away as personal vehicles supplanted much of the train's ridership.

The former Ballard's building was partitioned to provide spaces to more businesses. George Pollock's Crozet Variety Store, located where Crozet Hardware is today, carried many knick-knacks that one might have otherwise needed to travel to the big city to find. Pollock's marquee item, though, was *Freezer-Fresh Ice Cream*, made daily on the premises. The "Super-Creamed" treat debuted there in 1938 and a large sign advertising its availability hung over the sidewalk for many years. D. D. McGregor operated his insurance business next door, and a small restaurant existed upstairs for a brief period. Roy Barksdale's Electronics Unlimited store helped to transition the appeal of The Square from the days-of-old toward more modern times.

The Square's narrowest business-space was where one went for shoe and leather repairs for many years. Henry Smith, who owned several businesses in Crozet including the Crozet Theatre across the street from the Drug Store, started his shoe repair business on The Square and operated there before selling out to shoemaker Dan Bishop. Lester Washington, Smith's most apt apprentice in the 1930s, became Crozet's most recognized African-American businessman. Washington left the employ of Dan Bishop in 1949 to start his own Crozet Shoe Repair business which endured, in partnership with his wife Thelma, until their retirement in the early 1980s.

For many years the A&P Grocery store, later Red Front Market, operated beside the Crozet Drug Store. In 1949 its owner, Jack Wagner, was joined on The Square by his wife Nannie who operated the Red Front Five and Ten in the adjacent building. Their two businesses were connected internally via a walk-thru passageway—Crozet's first indoor mall!

The sounds of steam trains arriving and departing; horse's hooves and teamsters' shouts; the squeal of teenagers' tires; ice cream cones and fountain service—with a smile; excited chatter that filled the space when the movies let out; the cry of "Bingo!" from the fund-raising stand between The Square and Barnes Lumber Company; Christmas carols being sung 'round the towering old tree that marked the center of Crozet's public Square — each of these remembrances and so many others are recalled by the generations who have known the excitement and the comforts of that special place. May its heartbeat continue.

13

Greenwood, Virginia

The first depot at Greenwood was destroyed by Federal Cavalry during the Civil War. This modern station was the last to serve the rail traveler at that location.

Scattered along the foothills of western Albemarle County's Blue Ridge Mountains is a community which boasts a history unlike any other. An armchair ride through the storied annals of Greenwood, Virginia, reveals a place in time where a socio-economically diverse people co-existed with a respect for each other that transcended race and class.

The village's beginnings were rooted in a plantation settled by Isaac Hardin in 1785 that came to be called Greenwood by subsequent owners. Its future was forever altered when, in the 1850's, Claudius Crozet's Blue Ridge Railroad laborers dug out the eastern-most of four tunnels required to transport trains west through the mountains. Near the eastern portal to this 538' tunnel, Thomas C. Bowen, then owner of the former Hardin tract, gave a parcel of land for railroad use and a depot was established there. The depot and subsequent post office logically adopted the name "Greenwood."

Just like frontier stagecoach stops and modern interstate highway interchanges, early railroad depots were a magnet for commercial interests. The rail travelers whose passenger cars first paused at the Greenwood water tank were probably offered sandwiches or drinks through the open car windows. Within a short time, general stores and a hotel were erected nearby, accompanied by necessary services such as blacksmiths and liveries.

William Dinwiddie, a graduate of the University of Virginia, established the Brookland School, a preparatory academy, at Greenwood in 1856. The following year he moved the school to his home near the train station. But school day routines were severely interrupted when the Civil War came home.

Greenwood was a regular witness to troop movements during the Civil War. Confederate forces were often moved over the mountain by train, including Gen. Thomas J. "Stonewall" Jackson's secretive maneuvers during his Valley Campaign of 1862. Dinwiddie's school and grounds were taken over and used as a Confederate hospital, with nearly 800 sick and wounded soldiers accommodated there. The Dinwiddies nearly lost use of their home to similar purposes, per an order from C.S.A. Medical Director Hunter McGuire. The large family and their guests were spared this deprivation following urgent written appeals to Gen. Jackson and the Confederate Surgeon General.

During the 1870s, Tyree Dollins and Sons established a successful nursery business, shipping their young trees and plants from Greenwood Depot. Farmers and nurserymen benefited from the special soil qualities in the Piedmont foothills, and the mountainsides continued to fill with fruit trees and berries. The export market for the tariff-free Albemarle Pippin created a boon for local growers of this prized apple, and those in the Greenwood area were no exception.

The spectacular Mirador estate house was built in 1842 by merchant and miller James M. Bowen, brother of Thomas Bowen. When Chiswell Dabney Langhorne moved his family into Mirador in 1894, Greenwood stepped onto society's world stage for an extended season. Langhorne's affluence and social standing brought a steady stream of visitors to the halls of Mirador. With a private telephone line strung from Mirador to the rail station at Greenwood, Langhorne could stop the train at will for his guests, or receive direct notice of special shipments.

Mirador—and Greenwood—soon received even more attention because of the fame achieved by two of its adopted daughters, Langhorne sisters Irene and Nancy. Irene became the bride of

This 1880s stereoview of the east portal of Greenwood Tunnel was published by Anderson of Richmond, Virginia, in a series highlighting views along the C&O Railroad.

A.C. Bruce operated a store and mill adjacent to Greenwood Depot. A full service merchant, he offered groceries, shoes, hardware, stoves, furniture, farm implements, hay and feed, roofing, coal and wood.

well-known artist Charles Dana Gibson, and the inspiration for Gibson's famed "Gibson Girl" illustrations. Nancy's second marriage to Waldorf Astor led to her becoming the first woman to sit in the British House of Commons. Her wit and outspokenness brought her much attention and a degree of notoriety. She remained a sought-after figure whenever she returned to Virginia.

For decades Greenwood was renowned for glimpses of high-society figures, as newspapers reported who was seen arriving or departing at the train station. But it remained grounded as a community of regular folk making a living however they knew best.

The Greenwood neighborhood benefited from the philanthropy of its well-to-do citizens. The first public free school in the Greenwood area held classes in a log cabin on private land. Two successively larger school houses were eventually built. With an increased enrollment, additional teachers, and various improvements fostered by the Greenwood Community League, Greenwood became an accredited High School in 1920. Successful fund-raising and an interest-free loan from a local benefactor allowed the construction of a large, modern school which graduated its first class in 1922. Through the years, Greenwood School was home to several teachers—as well as a former student—who later became principals at other county schools. At least six of these principals went on to become Superintendent of Albemarle County Schools.

Greenwood Community Center, another evidence of community philanthropy, was opened in 1950 as a memorial to the servicemen of both World Wars. It featured a large indoor roller skating rink, bowling lanes, a swimming pool, ball diamond, restrooms and kitchen facilities. It stood high among Albemarle County recreational

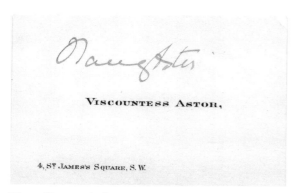

The calling card of Nancy Langhorne of Mirador, who married Waldorf Astor. When she won election to succeed him in the British House of Commons, she became the first woman to take her seat there.

facilities and was the direct result of hard work and fund-raising by progressive community members.

Several interesting volumes have been published on life in and around Greenwood: *Tears and Laughter in Virginia and Elsewhere*, by Ella Williams Smith; *Always a Virginian*, by Alice Winn; and *Memories of Greenwood School: 1921–1984*, by Steven Meeks—to name only a few.

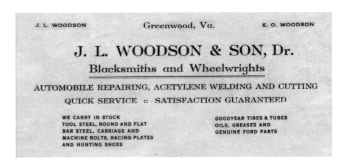

Blacksmiths in the early 20th century had to expand their skills to stay in business. The Woodsons at Greenwood adapted well, judging by their 1930s business letterhead.

Darrell J. Howard's recently published *Sunday Coming: Black Baseball in Virginia* includes wonderful interviews and remembrances from the African American communities in central Virginia. Howard recounts many exciting and nostalgic stories of the Black baseball teams from Greenwood—the Greenwood Athletic Club and the Greenwood Hawks—and of legendary ballplayers from the Sims family and others around the area.

Countless stories remain to be retold of earlier life in the Greenwood area: yarns from Bruce's, Young's, or Gill's Store, or Woodson's Blacksmith Shop; life in the Newtown section of Greenwood; the Summer Rest resort for young women; church life; mountain orchards....

The assimilation of once-unique neighborhoods and communities can be an unfortunate byproduct of "improvements" in transportation, or a shift in a local economy. Few rural villages can lay claim to a more diverse—and interesting—cultural background than western Albemarle County's Greenwood community.

Summer Rest, a "vacation house" built in 1896 by the Episcopal Diocese of Virginia, was an inexpensive mountain retreat established to serve employed women from Richmond.

14

Mechum's River, Virginia

An early view looking west toward Mechum's River Depot, located at milepost 192 on the Chesapeake and Ohio Railroad. [Photo courtesy of Ruby Starke Sandridge.]

To travelers passing through the community of Mechum's River, Virginia, things may seem relatively calm these days. But like an elderly neighbor dozing in a rocking chair, its quiet demeanor masks a vital, active past.

Archaeological digs conducted in the immediate area uncovered pre-historic tools and arrowheads. Evidences of a more recent Monacan Indian village were also uncovered and studied.

Eighteenth-century planters took full advantage of the verdant bottom lands of Mechum's River and reaped the rich profits of their exports. An ancient pathway used by Native-Americans was intersected at this place by late-18th and early 19th-century toll roads built to facilitate the transport of commodities from the Shenandoah Valley to markets east of the Blue Ridge Mountains.

The Reverend Edgar Woods published his *History of Albemarle County Virginia* in 1901. In regards to the naming of the river, he noted that it came "from a George Mechum, who was an owner of land near its head. The north fork of Mechum's was called Stockton's Creek, and its south fork, now regarded as the main stream, Stockton's Mill Creek, from a numerous family occupying their margins."

Oakridge School was one of the early schools that served children living in the Mechum's River area. Today it is a private residence. [Photo courtesy of Mac Sandridge.]

A three-stories-tall mill was located near the confluence of Lickinghole Creek and Mechum's River at an early date. It was this vital business—first called Jarman's Mill, and later, Walker's Mill—that lent these names to the early settlement. The crossroads community was already well-established by 1852 when the railroad arrived at the eastern precipice above the river. In 1854 a temporary track laid across Rockfish Gap finally connected the railroad east of the Blue Ridge with the rails extending westward across the Shenandoah Valley. The community was renamed Mechum's River Depot when mail service arrived by train.

In May, 2000, this writer was privileged to ride along with longtime Crozet resident Homer Sandridge (1916–2004) as he pointed out places of special interest along Brown's Gap Turnpike.

"The railroad came to Mechum's River before it stopped," Sandridge said as we paused near the site of the former train station at Mechum's River. "They had to wait until Claudius Crozet came along and built the tunnels. My earliest remembrance of what my daddy did—he was working on Mount Fair Farm up there—he along with two or three other people who worked on the farm were cutting telegraph poles. They were 45 or 50 feet long. Hauled them with a four-horse team to Mechum's River to put them on a train to ship them. At that time, you see, there was a railroad station at Crozet, but I think the road was better to Mechum's River. And this [depot] had been here longer so people were used to this being the station. From here [Mechum's River] to Brown's Gap is called the Brown's Gap Turnpike. That road was built through one of the openings from the valley to eastern Virginia early on."

Many are familiar with another May date—this one in 1862—when Confederate General Thomas J. "Stonewall" Jackson directed his troops through Brown's Gap and down the turnpike to Mechum's River Depot. As his soldiers encamped in the fields around Mechum's River, Jackson finalized his strategies in the hotel adjacent to the depot. While the spring-flowering dogwoods, redbuds and serviceberry trees bloomed all along the Blue Ridge foothills, Jackson orchestrated a series of brilliantly planned shuttle-rides on the Virginia Central Railroad through Claudius Crozet's mountain tunnels, cunningly transporting his thousands of foot soldiers back into the great Valley of Virginia. A series of masterful victories ensued, and the tactics, some of which were formed secretly in the railroad hotel room at Mechum's River, have been analyzed by military strategists ever since.

By springtime-1865 the fates of war had turned decidedly toward the Union side. Following a decisive victory over General Jubal Early's forces at Waynesboro, the Union Army, led by Generals Philip Sheridan and George Custer, followed the rail line east over the mountains, destroying the steel rails and burning all of the depots and bridges a considerable distance past Charlottesville, including, of course, those at Mechum's River. The carnage of this most un-civil war mercifully ended in April, 1865, and all began the difficult task of rebuilding their ravaged lives.

Betty Garwood Clayton, in her endearing 1999 book *Friends in High Places and Those Things We Hold Dear*, shared some of the remembrances penned by much-beloved and longtime Mechum's River resident Margaret Ragsdale. Ragsdale's recollections included many images of a vibrant community centered around its railroad depot. A water tank at the depot, required to replenish the early steam locomotives, was kept full by a nearby resident who ran a pump house

Dillard Sandridge drives his team up to the C&O Railroad siding at Mechum's River Depot to off-load a wagonload of sand he has dredged from the nearby river. [Photo courtesy of E.B. and Naomi Hicks.]

located where Lickinghole Creek emptied into the Mechum's.

A fenced "tie lot" near the depot allowed the penning of livestock that awaited shipment on the train. It also served as the "parking lot" where local train passengers could leave their steeds. Next to its gate was a large scale to weigh the "trade" of commercial shippers.

A short distance from the depot, adjacent to the west end of the railroad bridge spanning the high banks of the river, was a large hotel that alternately served as overnight accommodations for the traveling public, a boarding house and a summer resort.

Nearby were a public ice house, general store, post office, blacksmith shop and private dwellings. The first school serving Mechum's River was on a hill to the west, and farther beyond it was a plantation home that served as a "public house" to early turnpike travelers.

Among the earliest businesses in the community was the multi-storied water-powered mill built c.1790. Other businesses included a bark mill that processed the wagonloads of beneficial tree bark brought from the mountain forests. The bark mill eventually gave way to a cooper's shop/barrel factory that was lastly converted into a short-lived tomato cannery.

A Presbyterian congregation established a meeting house in the Mechum's River area during the early/mid 1700s. Before they departed in the early 1800s, a Baptist congregation began meet-

A letterhead from the Mechum's River Mill advertised: "High Grade Family Flour–Whole Wheat Flour–Hog, Chicken and Dairy Feeds–Stone Ground Corn Meal." It was destroyed by a fire in 1951. [Photo courtesy of Bill Clayton.]

ing nearby. Two different Baptist congregations still maintain houses of worship alongside a remnant of the old Three Notch'd Road. In an earlier day, their baptism ceremonies were often performed in the river near the mill.

Chaos rained down on the Mechum's River area during the afternoon of September 29, 1959, when remnants of Hurricane Gracie spawned a tornado that devastated many buildings throughout the region. The home and farm of John W. Clayton Jr. was especially hard-hit, and significant damage was wrought on Mountain Plain Baptist Church. Tragically, 11 persons were killed by the twisting winds just southeast of Mechum's River near Ivy. Ten of those fatalities were members of one family, including adults and young children.

Hundreds of good Samaritans quickly converged on the Mechum's River area and assisted with clean-up and rebuilding efforts. Near Lacey Spring in Rockingham County, across the Blue Ridge Mountains in the Shenandoah Valley—50 miles from Mechum's River—a water-stained bank note was found. It had been carried by remnants of the tornado winds that had snatched it from a desk in Clayton's hilltop home at Mechum's River. It was returned to the Clayton family just a few days later by the farmer who found it.

The Mechum's River community has experienced much life and more than its fair share of drama throughout its centuries of existence. Don't let its quiet repose today fool you.

Charles H. and Lillian (Sandridge) Coleman's general store at Mechum's River was one of three stores that operated concurrently there. Theirs was located on the roadfront between the depot and the mill. It was moved a short distance c.1917 to make way for the "new" road (present Rt. 240) from Crozet. [Photo courtesy of E.B. and Naomi Hicks.]

In 1959 Hurricane Gracie spawned a deadly tornado that seriously damaged a number of homes, farm buildings and a church in the Mechum's River area. Eleven people were killed near Ivy. [Photo courtesy of Bill Clayton.]

This smartly-dressed young fellow posed in the alleyway between the downtown cold storage facility and the C&O Railroad. The overhead walkway facilitated movement of ice and fruit between the storage plant and freight cars on the adjacent railway siding. The building in the background was the freight depot that sat across the tracks from Crozet's C&O passenger station. [Photo courtesy of Jimmy Belew.]

15

Mountainside: A Building for the Ages

Major structural renovations to the former Herbert Cold Storage facility continued during the winter of 1978-79. Today, Crozet's six-story high-rise is home to more than 100 residents.

Mountainside Senior Living stands tall in the heart of downtown Crozet, Virginia. The Jefferson Area Board for Aging—JABA—took over management of the assisted-living facility in 2002. Today, those fortunate to pass through its doors encounter a secure and caring community environment. Mountainside residents participate in the life of Crozet, and Crozet and western Albemarle County, in turn, are actively involved in the life of Mountainside.

The dramatic transformation of this historic, early-20th-century industrial plant into today's modern assisted-living oasis began with far-sighted renovations initiated by developer Stanley Wilcox in 1978. The resulting residential community, originally named Windham, opened in 1981.

The downtown cold storage plant's operations stretched from Crozet's Main Street all the way back to present day Carter Street, named to memorialize the plant's original owner. The facility's towering water tank, long a Crozet landmark, was razed in December 1978. [Photo by Mac Sandridge.]

Around the turn of the twentieth-century, two wood-framed buildings fronted the west side of Main Street next to the railroad. The one closest to the tracks was a private residence. Next door was Curtis A. Haden's general store.

At that time, the burgeoning fruit industry in western Albemarle County was producing more apples than could be sold and transported during the peak of harvest season. An association of local apple growers was organized to construct and operate a facility where excess fruit could be properly stored until sold. Steps were undertaken by this group to erect a cold storage warehouse.

The selected site placed this new enterprise in the center of Crozet's growing downtown business district. Convenient access for loading railcars necessitated the removal of the private residence next to the tracks. This was

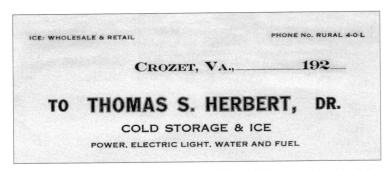

ICE: WHOLESALE & RETAIL   PHONE NO. RURAL 4-0-L

CROZET, VA.,_____ 192__

TO THOMAS S. HERBERT, DR.

COLD STORAGE & ICE

POWER, ELECTRIC LIGHT, WATER AND FUEL

Thomas Herbert took over operation of the cold storage plant built by W.F. Carter. The massive facility alongside the C&O tracks in the center of Crozet provided refrigerated storage for the region's abundant apple crops, ice for homes and businesses, plus electricity and running water to the surrounding village. [Image courtesy of Crozet Print Shop.]

accomplished by jacking up and gently moving the two-story house several hundred yards north—across the train tracks—where it still stands nearly 100 years later. This is the same house where, in October 1978, James Crosby began publishing his Crozet-based newspaper *The Bulletin of Western Albemarle County*. Interestingly, the front page story in The Bulletin's first issue reported the proposal to renovate Crozet's old cold storage building into an adult health care facility.

The fruit growers' collective efforts bogged down during the early stages of construction, and the project was taken over by three Crozet business men. In March 1910, William F. Carter, C. L. Wayland, and W. F. Carter Jr. filed a charter with the Clerk of Albemarle County for the Crozet Ice and Cold Storage Corporation. Their intentions, according to the charter, were to "… manufacture, buy and sell ice and any other goods, wares and merchandise; to operate a refrigerating plant or plants, with storehouse, warehouse, and other facilities, with the right to receive for storage, refrigeration and safe keeping any and all goods …"

Additions to the plant in 1912 and 1919 created the lasting landmark we still recognize today. In the 1920s, Thomas S. Herbert bought the business and renamed it Herbert Cold Storage and Ice Company, Inc. Herbert promoted his facility as having a cold storage capacity of 450,000 cubic feet, and the capability to produce 40 tons of ice daily. The company promoted the sale of "ice refrigerators at cost" to a rural population mostly unreached by electrical service. As a mem-

Carter's (later, Herbert's) Cold Storage plant provided year-round employment for a number of local men. Their shovels were kept busy feeding the plant's coal-fired engines. [Photo courtesy of Mac Sandridge.]

The sweeping outdoor stairway leading to the entrance of Mountainside Senior Living ascends from the space once occupied by the auditorium of Crozet Theatre.

ber of the International Apple Shippers Association, the company's motto was "Apples for Health – all the year 'round."

During its heyday, the Cold Storage plant was a beneficial presence in the Crozet community. It provided a variety of year-'round jobs in an otherwise seasonal economy. Clerical, sales, production and maintenance workers were joined during busy seasons by part-time laborers and high-schoolers with strong backs. The plant's railway siding included a coal drop to supply the facility's power-producing engines, also making that commodity more convenient for local businesses and homes.

A dramatic event occurred in the late 1940s when the adjoining Crozet Theater, converted from Haden's Store in 1938, caught fire. The daytime blaze broke out near the theater's furnace, located behind the stage, and went unnoticed until the building was at great risk of loss. Members of the Crozet Volunteer Fire Department were summoned from their jobs in area businesses by the wail of the siren atop the fire station. When the first responders entered the theater's auditorium through the Main Street entrance to attack the fire with their fire hoses, they encountered a wall of flames rapidly advancing from the stage area. The intensity and danger of the situation soon drove them back outside, and it was decided that the only hope for saving the structure was to haul their hoses onto the flat roof of the six-story Cold Storage to fight the blaze from above. Although the theater suffered major damage, a total loss was prevented by the quick, bold actions of Crozet's hometown fire fighters and their precarious angle of attack delivered from the roof of the neighboring high-rise.

A changing local economy finally brought a close to the diversified interests of the Cold

This mid-1920s street-level view across The Square in downtown Crozet shows C.A. Haden's general store nestled alongside Herbert's Cold Storage facility. Haden's Store was converted into the Crozet Theatre in the late-1930s.

Storage. The region's fruit industry waned as an increasing number of local industries offered stable employment with fringe benefits. Electrification in rural areas signaled the last days of manufactured ice for cooling purposes.

The ensuing years saw only sporadic activity around the quiet structure, including curious youth occasionally prowling through its dark recesses. For a brief season, organized indoor "shooting matches," open to the public, were held in one of the storage facility's cavernous rooms. Competing for prizes and/or cash pots, sporting individuals attempted to prove the superiority of their aim with a shotgun in the deafening, smoke-filled confines.

Later, the Crozet Boxing Club was organized by several local men interested in harnessing and redirecting the energies of area youth, and instilling in them a spirit of good sportsmanship through the disciplines of competitive boxing. The club's gym, outfitted with a boxing ring and bleachers for spectators, was set up inside one of the storage plant's lower rooms.

Not many years later, the winds of change brought life-enhancing light into the darkened old facility. With the former industrial plant's spectacular transformation into a modern assisted-living facility, the vision of Wilcox and others stands prominently as a grand testimony to adaptive reuse.

Today Mountainside Senior Living is one of Crozet's largest employers. Its caring staff is key to the family environment provided to more than 100 residents. And where else can be enjoyed such unique sweeping views of Albemarle County's Piedmont foothills!

The Venerable Frederick William Neve, D.D., (1855–1948), was a priest of the Episcopal Church in the Diocese of Virginia. While serving congregations at Ivy and Greenwood, he established numerous mission outposts in the Blue Ridge Mountains of Albemarle, Greene, Madison, Page and Rockingham Counties.

16

The Archdeacon of the Blue Ridge

The first centrally located mission workers' house established by Archdeacon Neve was built in 1903 on the Albemarle and Greene County line. This mountain crossroads location grew to include a school, church, hospital, clothing bureau, Preventorium and post office—appropriately designated Mission Home.

When the church bells tolled at St. Paul's Episcopal Church in Ivy on November 16, 1948, their mournful peals reverberated up through the hollows and across the ridges of the Blue Ridge Mountains. The mountain inhabitants had lost a best friend and champion; Christendom, a model servant.

The congregants at St. Paul's Church had found themselves in dire need of a rector some 60 years earlier. Many of St. Paul's parishioners were of English descent and they desired a leader from the Old Country. Together with the assembly at Emmanuel Episcopal Church near Greenwood, they invited, without success, more than a half-dozen ministers. Through advertisement followed by an on-site search in England, a willing candidate was finally found. William Frederick Neve, the Oxford graduate who accepted their call at the age of 32, had spent the majority of his six years in the priest-hood ministering directly to the poor and laboring class.

Although the congregations at Ivy and Greenwood were quite satisfied with their new clergyman, he found his work within the two middle-class congregations slightly less than fulfilling. His greater desire was to be useful in missionary endeavors.

Ivy's nearby Ragged Mountains soon provided Neve with the opportunity for missionary service which he sought. Slowly earning the confidence of these more isolated families within his parish area, he eventually found acceptance among them, and determined to build a simple chapel in close proximity to their homes. When the fund raising efforts of his primary congregations fell short of the amount required to build and outfit the rural chapel, Neve faced the first of the numerous financial challenges his "mountain mission" work would encounter.

At his critical hour of need, Neve received a letter from his father in England informing him of a small sum of money just discovered within his financial books—prior savings that were owed to Neve. It proved to be the amount required to complete the mission chapel.

Neve had discovered his divine calling. On November 1st, 1890, an overflow crowd of more than 100

THE ORDER
of the
THOUSANDFOLD

PRAYER OF THE ORDER.

Almighty God, our Heavenly Father, Who with Thy Son Jesus Christ hast given unto us all things in heaven and earth, we beseech Thee to make us a thousandfold more useful to Thee than ever before, so that Thy power and blessing may flow through us to multitudes of others who are in need, and also make us more willing and loving servants of Thine to Thy honor and glory for Jesus Christ's sake. Amen.

Archdeacon Neve and his young daughter Helen reenacted the moment which had inspired Neve to found his Order of the Thousandfold in 1920, encouraging others to "pray without ceasing" and to pray to be 1000 times more useful to the Kingdom of God. [Pamphlet courtesy of Larry Lamb.]

attended a service of dedication for the new building. During the service, Neve memorialized his mother who had died when he was only 13, and named the new place of worship for St. John the Baptist who had proclaimed the coming of the Lord in the wilderness.

Always looking forward, never satisfied only with where he had been, Neve, in addition to caring for his home congregations, spent his energies publicizing the needs that could be met in the isolated pockets of the Blue Ridge Mountains. He traveled far and wide, wherever he could obtain an invitation, showing pictures and telling first-person stories of the mountain mission work. He solicited funds for the building of mountain schools and for the hiring of their teachers. He took on seminary students and introduced them to the work.

His goal was to locate points for mission work at ten mile intervals along the Blue Ridge Mountains. He eventually accomplished that and much more. In 1904 the position of "Archdeacon of the Blue Ridge" was created by the Episcopal Diocese of Virginia, and Archdeacon Neve became the overseer of the work. By the time he resigned as rector of St. Paul's-Ivy (after 35 years of service to the congregation who had initially called him to America), his promotion of the mountain work was occupying most of his days.

Neve's vision had been "*to bring to bear on an isolated people the full power of the Gospel, that they may have that more abundant life which Our Lord came to give, and that the youth of the mountains may become leaders in Church and State.*" By 1932 there was much to bear witness to its effectiveness and success: 30 missions, 12 day schools, one Industrial Boarding School, 12 clergy, 46 lay workers, and 1300 communicants, and a Preventorium for the building up of children at risk of developing tuberculosis. Through the years, other bold leaders assumed many of the responsibilities of the day-to-day care of the various districts into which the mountain work had been divided. Those who stepped forward to live and work in the isolated outposts were legion, as were

Archdeacon Neve paused with parishioners on the porch at St. John the Baptist Chapel in the Ragged Mountains near Ivy, Virginia. He had just performed baptism rites for seven babies and one adult.

Uncle Billy and Aunt America—William and America Jane (Sullivan) Garrison—opened their cabin home, beginning in 1900, to mission workers of the Simmon's Gap School built on the mountaintop at the Greene and Rockingham County line. [Image courtesy of Earl Sullivan.]

the innumerable small and large financial supporters of the work.

Through the vision of one man and the efforts of many, lives were changed for the better in the mountains. But by the 1930s, even more radical changes were taking place. Much of Neve's 100-mile-long mission field was being assumed by the newly-created Shenandoah National Park. Families, homes, schools, churches—a way of life—were being forced off the mountains.

The mountain mission work continued at other locations, but many of the needs of the previous half-century had been met. By the 1940s those still involved in the work remained as dedicated as the earlier workers had been. The unique Archdeaconry of the Blue Ridge had become a model that was studied and adapted in other places. Neve's personal work evolved into his writings—a way he could still share his wisdom, knowledge and inspiration with a new generation of church leadership.

The Tanner's Ridge mission school was located on the mountaintop in Page County, a short distance from Shenandoah National Park's Big Meadows development. During the trying days of World War II, Tanner's Ridge school teacher Janet Walton happily announced via the pages of Neve's *Our Mountain Work* newsletter that her students, "by different ones contributing small amounts," were sponsoring a British child during the year 1943. The children's sacrificial giving demonstrated the full-circle fruits of the missionary laborers and the financial supporters near and far who had helped make possible the work among the mountain residents.

Not long following Frederick Neve's death in 1948 at the age of 93, the "official" Archdeaconry was incorporated under the banner of the Diocesan Department of Missions. The 60-year work of the once-tireless priest from the County of Kent, England, came to an official close.

Those who remember Archdeacon Neve would concur with Crozet resident Pauline Corbin who summed up her own recollections for this writer by saying, "Rev. Neve was a great man. He really was a great man."

Christmas was observed and celebrated throughout the mountain missions with special programs put on by the local children. Simple gifts were distributed and home-prepared refreshments were enjoyed by all in attendance. In Blackwell's Hollow, Freeman and Marie Fisk, workers at St. John's Mission, penned this verse in observance of the Christmas season. Their heartfelt words mirrored the message that William Frederick Neve spent his lifetime demonstrating:

> *'Tis not enough that Christ was born*
> *Beneath the star that shown,*
> *And earth was set that morn*
> *Within a golden zone.*
> *He must be born within the heart*
> *Before He finds his throne,*
> *And brings the day of love and good—*
> *The reign of Christlike brotherhood.*

This "new concrete and metal schoolhouse" at "Simmon's Gap, VA" was built in 1911 with donations from supporters of the mountain mission work. It replaced the earlier wooden structure provided by Neve in 1901.

A young boy sits astride a hobby horse and watches as workers assemble the three-abreast Herschell-Spillman carousel on the midway of Bruce Greater Shows. The Rudolph Wurlitzer band organ, visible behind the white horse, filled depression-era midways with happy melodies. [Photo courtesy of Dennis Davis.]

17

Queen of the Carousel

Bruce's Carnival grew from a single, early-1900s merry-go-round into a sizeable tent city that required as many as 20 railcars to transport its equipment and employees. [Photo courtesy of Dennis Davis.]

A little girl destined to bring joy to many was born in the remote Blue Ridge foothills of northwestern Albemarle County a few weeks following the close of America's tragic Civil War. When she sat down with Albemarle historian Vera Via in the 1950s, her eyes still sparkled as she recalled some of the events from her long, active life.

Lucy Mildred Walton was born in the spring of 1865, the tenth child of Minceberry ('Berry) Walton (a blacksmith well-respected in the area around the crossroads village of Boonesville, Virginia) and Lucy Hall (also from a family long-settled in that area). She grew up to be called Lucy Millie by those who knew her best.

South and southwest of Boonesville, as appears on the 1866 Albemarle County map drawn by noted Civil War cartographer Jed Hotchkiss, are Bruce's Mountain and Bruce's Hollow. George W. Bruce, a member of the family for whom these geographical features were named, married Lucy Millie Walton in 1881. When Berry Walton died in 1886, his son John T. Walton took over the blacksmith business. Then, in 1904, George Bruce bought his brother-in-law's blacksmith shop and 52 surrounding acres, and established himself in the retail business. The intersecting roads that led local traffic to Bruce's Boonesville Store would soon serve to transport George and Lucy Millie far afield from their Blue Ridge Mountain home: in the early 1900's, they established a carnival.

ROUTE BOOK
1930 Season
Bruce Greater Shows
"*America's Greatest Exposition*"
Jim Henry Bruce

JAMES H. BRUCE
Owner & Manager

Mrs. J. H. Bruce
Secretary & Treasurer

C. W. Cracraft
General Representative

Roy B. Jones
Special Representative

George Parrott
Superintendent

Charles Randall
Chief Electrician

Raleigh Gibson
Foreman of Rides

Russell Lane
Trainmaster

Prof. Harold Benson
Musical Director

Jim Henry Bruce (1884–1935) insisted that the carnival's shows provide clean, family entertainment. His management and promotional talents were honed by the Christian character of his parents. [Photo courtesy of Dennis Davis.]

The earliest years of George and Lucy Millie's entertainment business venture were spent in relatively local environs. They opened their first season at Gordonsville, Virginia, with only a carousel, or, as Lucy Millie related to writer/historian Vera Via, "one set of hobby horses."

The work required to transport and set up even that one amusement ride was no small feat in the beginning decades of the 1900s. The motorized transportation industry was in its infancy and the rural highways were still little more than improved wagon roads. Nevertheless, the Bruces persevered with the assistance of several family members, and gradually added more midway features and amusement rides. Several of their Boonesville-area neighbors signed on to help as the traveling show expanded.

Bruce's Boonesville Store continued to operate despite the Bruces' seasonal absences. After the carnival's final engagement in the fall, its equipment was returned to Boonesville where it was carefully stored away until the following spring.

George and Lucy Millie Bruce, with monumental hard work and sound business principles, grew their operation into a formidable traveling enterprise. It advanced beyond a carnival solely transported by trucks into a business that booked engagements mainly along the rail lines that transported much of its equipment and personnel. When Jim Henry Bruce was handed the management reins by his father in 1926, Bruce's Carnival had garnered ample respect in the industry and in the towns where they appeared. The Bruce's clean, family-oriented shows and amusements regularly received return invitations from their sponsoring hosts.

Along with the subtle change in management came a business name change that reflected its status in the industry. Bruce's Carnival officially became Bruce Greater Shows. Its range of travel extended from upstate New York to Georgia.

When the carnival set up for a rare two-week engagement at the Belmont Show Grounds in Charlottesville, Virginia, at the beginning of the 1927 show season, the local news media reported daily on the big event. "BIGGER AND BETTER THAN EVER", touted the Daily Progress advertisements and write-ups. "Founded on the slogan and watchword 'class, cleanliness and character'… the Bruce name has become synonymous with clean amusement." As was typical of promotions in that day, Bruce also advertised that "200

Playing beside one of the Bruce Greater Shows private railroad cars, this youngster was raised on the sawdust trail. [Photo courtesy of Dennis Davis.]

people" were required to put on the show. In later years that number grew to 400—a far cry from the small group of family and neighbors who had moved George and Lucy Millie's first set of hobby-horses the 30 miles from Boonesville to Gordonsville.

Bruce Greater Shows, like all traveling operations of its size, regularly picked up and dropped off laborers as the show relocated and the season progressed. One such roustabout who hired on with Bruce Greater Shows around 1929 or '30 was a young Dutchman named Andre van Kuijk. He had arrived recently in the United States, hardly able to speak English, and desperately needing work. The country was already sliding head-first into the Great Depression and jobs were hard to come by, even for those with good local connections.

Fortunately for van Kuijk, he was not a complete stranger to carnival life: he had worked as a young boy for small change in the carnivals and fairs that visited his hometown. He signed on

Born in Boonesville, Virginia, Lucy Millie Walton Bruce (1865–1962) relished her role as matriarch of the traveling carnival managed by her hard-working family. [Photo courtesy of Dennis Davis.]

with the first carnival he came across and quickly assimilated into the family of working travelers. Andre van Kuijk soon saw the need to adopt an American name and began to call himself Tom Parker. As Parker, he worked his way onto several different show circuits, learning the wisdom and skills of those with whom he worked, and honing his own unique style from lessons he learned on the road. Those who knew him were not surprised when, years later, he chose the showman's moniker of "Colonel". When Colonel Tom Parker was singled out for honor by the Showmen's League of America in 1994, he proudly listed Bruce Greater Shows near the top of his list of "career affiliations." This same Colonel Tom Parker was best known for managing and promoting a singing truck driver from Memphis named Elvis.

In company with Vera Via, Lucy Millie shared wistfully her love for the carnival circuit in spite of its demanding hardships. In 1933 George Bruce passed away. As matriarch of her family at home and her carnival family on the road, Lucy Millie kept a hand in the operations of the family's business. Tragedy struck again only three years later, just weeks prior to the beginning of the 1935 season. Jim Henry Bruce, perhaps worn down from the rigors of carnival travel, succumbed following a brief illness. Bruce Greater Shows had lost its greatest promoter, but the new season was already booked: it was decided that the show must go ahead.

Working through her sorrow at the age of 70, Lucy Millie partnered with her newly-widowed daughter-in-law Margaret to keep the show going. Even with a faithful supporting staff, the burden of their collective grief was too great and the show eventually returned home to Boonesville. George Parrott, former Superintendent for Bruce Greater Shows, reorganized a portion of the show and returned to the road for a while, but the handwriting on the wall announcing the end proved true. The carnival's equipment was sold and Bruce Greater Shows was relegated

Albemarle County natives George and Lucy Millie Bruce stand at the ticket booth near their first carousel. [Photo courtesy of Dennis Davis.]

to the living memories of Lucy Millie and those who had labored alongside her.

During the brighter years when Bruce's Carnival returned to Boonesville at the end of its travel season, and before securing the carousel for the winter, George and Lucy Millie reassembled the three-abreast hobby horses one more time. They readied the carousel's decorated Wurlitzer Band Organ with its 164 wooden pipes and invited the Boonesville neighborhood for the season's last ride. The musical notes from the organ's pipes and bells mixed once more with the squeals of glee from the local children. And Lucy Millie's eyes surely sparkled as she gazed about at the autumn-leaved hillsides and pondered the joys of her blessed life.

18

Paul Clayton—Songcatcher

The view from the kitchen window in Paul Clayton's mountain cabin features the log shelter protecting the cabin's natural water source.

A friendly fellow once heralded as "the most recorded young folk singer" in America established a home base in the Blue Ridge Mountains of Albemarle County, Virginia, in the mid-1950s. From that rustic place of sanctuary and repose, he traveled the country and the world, established countless friendships along the way, and resurrected old songs nearly lost to the ages. Neither his name nor his midrange baritone voice is easily recognized today, but versions of the songs he brought back into the light are still enjoyed the world over.

New England native Paul Clayton Worthington grew up in the former whaling town of New Bedford, Massachusetts, where his maternal ancestors the Hardys had been connected with the whaling industry. The town's historic lore and his family's stories of those earlier associations intrigued Paul, and he set about to learn and record the musical traditions of the laboring mariners. In his early teen years, Worthington presented regular radio programs in his hometown of New Bedford and on Prince Edward Island, Canada, where his family vacationed in the summer.

In 1949 Paul enrolled in the University of Virginia. His English professor, Dr. Arthur Kyle Davis Jr., was a folklorist, and collected ballads from the natives of the nearby Blue Ridge Mountains. Davis had worked with U.Va. English professor C. Alphonso Smith, who, in 1916, introduced Cecil J. Sharp, a world-renowned ballad collector from England, to the local mountains and coves. There, rich repositories of old ballads still existed in the memories of the inhabit-

Marybird Bruce McAllister was a colorful singer of traditional mountain ballads. She accompanied herself on a banjo made in Beech Creek, North Carolina, purchased on a southern ballad collecting trip by Paul Clayton and Roger Abrahams. This 1960 photo was taken by George Foss.

ants. Professor Davis was deeply devoted to the ballad and to those who carried on the oral singing tradition, and it was he who encouraged young Worthington along the way.

During his first semester at U.Va., Paul met with several other students, most notably William Marburg, and they formed a music group playing old standards in the bluegrass style. Performing under the stage name *Bill Clifton*, Marburg established his own daily radio show at Charlottesville's WCHV radio station. Paul hosted a weekly program at competing station WINA, performing under the name *Paul Clayton*. They would occasionally collaborate on Clifton's early-morning program, billing themselves as *The Clifton Brothers, Harvey and Bill*.

In May of 1950, Paul used the WINA studio to record African-American bluesman Pinkney "Pink" Anderson (1900–1974) who was performing locally in a traveling carnival. (The English rock band *Pink Floyd* adopted their name from the colorful moniker of the former medicine show entertainer from South Carolina whose impromptu Charlottesville recording session—his first since 1928—was released by Riverside Records in 1961.)

The next several years were filled with tremendous activity: Clayton obtained his English degrees, and established himself as a respected folk musician throughout the eastern states, especially within the New York folk scene centered around Greenwich Village. He collected ballads in several European countries and recorded a series of television programs comparing British and American folksongs for the British Broadcasting Corporation. In 1956, he released six albums on three different record labels. He was a regular performer at Izzy Young's Folklore Center—ground-zero for "folkniks" in NYC.

One of the more fortuitous routes Clayton took was to the Blue Ridge foothills and Brown's Cove. He was introduced to ballad singer and banjoist Marybird Bruce McAllister. Born in 1877,

Marybird had a repertoire of more than 150 old songs. She lived with Al and Hilma Yates in a remote old log-bodied house, a popular stopping-in place for their mountain neighbors and extended family members. In the autumn of '56, Paul made a $600 investment that would return untold dividends: he purchased a primitive cabin on three acres of mountain land a short distance up the rutted trail from Al and Hilma Yates—and Marybird.

The cabin became Paul's private refuge from the rigors of travel and performing. With no electricity or running water, it provided rustic ambiance for writing and composing. The home served as a *close-in* base for in-depth Appalachian ballad collecting—and a *far-out* location for partying with his ample supply of friends. Many of those visiting friends helped make the old cabin more comfortable. They chinked logs, built a new outhouse, and added a log kitchen.

Paul's college friend and recording artist Bill Clifton used the mountain cabin as a backdrop for several of his album covers.

Folklorist and singer Roger Abrahams met Paul in New York's Greenwich Village. They made almost monthly trips to Virginia in 1957 and '58, putting on concerts at colleges along the way and in folk venues in Washington, D.C.

"We always stopped by to see Ma'ybird and Al and Hilma before we went up the road," Abrahams recalled. "It was in their parlor that I first sat and talked and sang in the approved mountain etiquette of interaction."

Paul Clayton sang in countless coffeehouses during his career as a folksinger in the 1950s and '60s. Caffè Lena, in Saratoga Springs, NY, opened in 1960 and is billed as "the oldest continuously operating coffeehouse in the United States." *Above right:* Clayton recorded this single in 1959 and included it on his album "Homemade Songs and Ballads" in 1961. Bob Dylan rewrote the lyrics—originally sung to Paul Clayton by Marybird McAllister—and in 1963 it became one of Dylan's signature hits.

Al and Hilma Yates relaxed near the woodstove in their secluded home in the Blue Ridge Mountains of Albemarle County, Virginia. George Foss photographed them during a visit in 1962.

George Foss connected with Paul Clayton after hearing Clayton on a Washington, D.C., radio interview. Foss, who was at that time playing cornet in the National Symphony Orchestra, joined Paul and others on their ballad collecting trips to the Blue Ridge Mountains. Like Paul, Foss also preserved many of those mountain visits on audio tape, and he later wrote of his experiences in his book *From White Hall to Bacon Hollow.*

Although great commercial success eluded Paul Clayton, he was well-respected in the early folk singing community. Many of those singers found their way to his secluded cabin, including Bob Dylan, who later recalled the bare necessities at Paul's cabin and its mirrored kerosene lanterns. On one such trip in the early 1960s, Clayton, Dylan and Joan Baez visited Charlottesville's Gaslight Restaurant.

George Foss pondered the life of his friend Paul Clayton, during an autumn visit to Clayton's cabin near Cedar Mountain in Brown's Cove.

Marybird's musical repertoire was a source of amazement for those who chanced to know her. It was a source of inspiration for Paul Clayton. One of her songs spoke images of a prisoner, lamenting that he "lay around, play around" on the chain gang until "summer come and gone, winter coming on." Paul's rewrite of her lyrics turned into the number-one country single "Gotta Travel On" for Billy Grammer in 1959. The big hit has since been sung by countless other artists.

Another ballad that Marybird sang for Paul asked, "Who Will Buy Your Chickens When I'm Gone?" Again Paul rephrased the lyrics and, in 1959, recorded "Whose Gonna Buy You Ribbons (When I'm Gone)." Bob Dylan heard Paul performing the song and decided to rework the tune himself. In 1963 Dylan's folk-rock classic "Don't Think Twice, It's Alright" was recorded—a world away from Marybird and the Yates' simple mountain home.

Folk music evolved slowly into the mainstream in the 1960s; changes were resisted by song traditionalists but embraced by the buying public. A few folksingers adapted and realized some commercial success. Fortunately for most folk musicians, commercialism wasn't their goal.

Paul Clayton was part of the folk music community in its infancy, but, despite his experience within the recording industry, he was unable to ride its wave of popularity. His many friends around the world and in the secluded coves of Appalachia were saddened in 1967 to learn of his ultimate despair and untimely death in New York City.

The gentle young singer is still revered today by those who knew him. Many of them would probably agree with the inscription beneath his portrait, kept by the family of his professor and friend, Dr. A. K. Davis Jr.: *Amongst the songs he sang for everyone did no one hear the song he sang alone.*

19
Mountain Spirits

Much historic symbolism, including an image of a primitive still, was included in this steel engraving that adorned the Internal Revenue's Special Stamp for a 1903 Nelson County retailer.

Have you ever walked the fire trail alongside the south fork of Moorman's River in Sugar Hollow, heading to Blue Hole for an invigorating plunge into its cool depths? Perhaps you and your family have turned off the Appalachian Trail at Jarman's Gap to enjoy the autumn colors of our beautiful Blue Ridge Mountains. If you have spent time on this antique mountain road, you undoubtedly noticed several signs of past human habitation. Leveled areas along both sides of the road contain chimneys and stone foundations that testify to the displacement of Albemarle County families prior to the establishment of Shenandoah National Park in the late 1930s.

My special interest in this mountain road was kindled during a 1999 visit with one of the last of Sugar Hollow's lifelong residents, the late Cecil McAllister. Cecil related to me how his father, Jim McAllister (1850–1935), had once worked at a distillery that had been located on the east side of the road near Blue Hole.

"My father used to make whiskey up at John Ballard's Stillhouse", Cecil said. "He worked there until Ballard started to add lye to it to make it hold a bead. That's when he quit and refused to work for him any more."

Ballard's Distillery appears on Green Peyton's 1875 *Map of Albemarle County, Virginia.* In the years prior to and immediately following the Civil War, Peyton, an 1849 UVa graduate with a degree in Civil Engineering, surveyed the county, recording the locations of almost 1300 businesses, churches, schools and prominent landowners. Included in that number were no less than 20 distilleries, with over half of these licensed operations located in the western mountain foothills.

Much lore has surrounded the manufacturing of alcoholic spirits, especially in the southern Appalachian Mountains. Alcoholic beverages were not developed by Native Americans in Virginia. The first Europeans brought rum imported from the Caribbean. Early settlers brewed beer and tried with little success to use native fox grapes to make wine. Once the early fruit orchards were developed, a part of their fruit production was converted into cider and fermented for brandy.

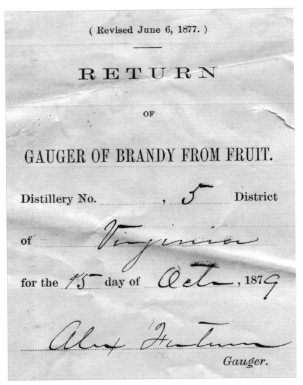

Adam Lowery's Fruit Distillery was monitored by government gauger Alex Fortune in 1879. The gauger certified each step of the distiller's processes.

It didn't take long for our fledgling government to institute regulations of all sorts. For the legal distiller, obeying the law meant paying fees for licenses as well as submitting to regular monitoring by a gauger, an official who analyzed and recorded the contents of every cask. This moni-

Prior to Prohibition, legally produced alcoholic liquors could be sold in Virginia by private "Retail Liquor Dealers". This ornate masthead is from a 1903 license for a central Virginia retailer. Following Prohibition's repeal, state liquor sales came under the jurisdiction of the Department of Alcoholic Beverage Control.

toring resulted in all of the required taxes being paid, from the fruit grower selling his produce to the distiller, down the chain to the retailer who was licensed to sell to the consumer.

Shaver's Distillery in Nelson County was licensed to distill only apples, peaches and grapes. Their monthly Internal Revenue return for September 1885 listed eight orchardists in the Avon and Greenfield area from whom they had purchased apples; the actual quantities of those raw materials; the number of hours each batch had been worked; the number of boilings in each still; and the final number of gallons of brandy distilled. A gauger's return dated September 1879 for Lowery's Distillery, one of Shaver's competitors, showed a total of 180 gallons of 100-proof peach, apple and grape brandy—with $162 of total tax owed.

This antique bullet-ridden relic was confiscated by ABC agents and briefly displayed on the Albemarle County courthouse lawn. [Photo by Mac Sandridge.]

So… how do *you* think an enterprising fellow might reduce the paperwork and avoid the taxman, if he was of a mind to try? With minimal capital, a bit of daring, and a lot of hard, manual labor, some small-time entrepreneurs chose to risk fines and imprisonment to make a little cash in the barter societies in which many of them lived. The illegal distilleries—moonshine stills—that they operated required a good water source, seclusion, and raw materials that could be transported on a strong back.

Several years ago I rode through the Brown's Cove area of western Albemarle with a former resident who had grown up in that community during the days of Prohibition. When I asked about moonshining, this is what was shared with me:

"I'm not saying this out of disrespect—some made a living making whiskey—and made a pretty good living in the twenties and thirties up here. And really, having lived up here, I could understand their doing this, because that was their way of getting what they needed. I remember up where we used to pasture our cows at in the summer—they [the cows] swarmed over a big territory—we have run across barrels of mash. See, these people would go to the store and buy a hundred pounds of sugar. Buy rye. See, they used rye—sugar and water and rye is what made the malt—the mash that they distilled. It fermented out of that. The general stores sold these people their supplies, really. Fruit jars—to put the finished product in. The sugar. The brown sugar, mainly, then. Brown was cheaper. It wasn't refined as much but it did just as well. Lye—for the grain, as I remember... It was mainly rye moonshine whiskey is what it was. When you learned to know those people you saw a lot of good in them. They weren't as bad a people as they portrayed the image of. That's the way I found them. They were very private people and they didn't trust strangers. They couldn't. But once they learned to know you and trust you—I called them good people, most of them."

Some orchardists, such as Bob Via, who lived with his family in a comfortable home near the headwaters of the north fork of Moorman's River, established very profitable, legal distilling operations. This seasonal supplement to Via's orcharding, cattle-raising and timbering enterprises, helped provide the means for him to hire lawyers and to challenge the right of the Commonwealth to confiscate his homeland to establish a national park. Losing his legal challenge at the State level, Via appealed to the U.S. Supreme Court. That court ultimately refused to hear his case.

Bob Via, like many of his mountain neighbors, was forced to move his family off their Albemarle County mountain lands. Today, the only physical evidences remaining that hint at the generations who once lived and thrived all along our Blue Ridges are a few scattered, overgrown foundations. Please remember our ancestral mountain neighbors with respect as you pass by.

The stone remnants of Ballard's Distillery stand silently beside a small stream that joins the south fork of Moorman's River in western Albemarle's Sugar Hollow.

20

The Library of Crozet

Several of the various "homes" of the Crozet Library are shown in this 1950s view: 1) John T. O'Neill's Store, which has also housed a car dealership, farm supply store, and the Green Olive Tree Thrift Store. 2) Chesley A. Haden & Co., originally a fruit brokerage office building. 3) C&O Railway Depot—the library's home since 1984. [Photo by Mac Sandridge.]

Where in the world is the Crozet Library?

What a silly question! Why, everyone knows it's bursting at its seams inside the former train depot alongside the railroad tracks in downtown Crozet. And, besides, the question on everyone's mind today is, "Where is the Crozet Library *going*?"

An accounting of where the library has *been*, though, reads like an intimate history of the village itself.

A record of Crozet's first library has been preserved by the Woman's Club of Crozet, though the library's genesis pre-dates the establishment even of that stalwart group. It is clearly evident that, through the years, it was the concerned women of the area who persisted in maintaining such a literary advantage for their town.

In 1907, Miss Dorothy Earp of nearby Yancey Mills was given a large variety of books from influential friends in Philadelphia who hoped Miss Earp might find them useful in her life's work of caring for patients in her home. Being overwhelmed with the quantity of books received, she encouraged the assistance of a teenage girl in her care to help set up a lending library in Crozet.

One of Crozet's first business men, "James M. Ellison: Dealer in Dry Goods, Notions, Groceries, & Shoes," had a feed shop near his mercantile on The Square. Ellison rented a storage room adjoining the shop to Miss Earp for two dollars a month.

"Such a funny, forlorn little old room," recalled Dorothy Earp, "with one window in the front and one in the back, with rough wooden boards by way of shutters, and with an un-planed and very dirty floor."

The floor was scrubbed and matting was tacked down over it. Unpainted boards were installed as book shelves. The windows, washed clean, were adorned with white ruffled curtains. The space was outfitted with a "little pig" stove for warmth. A desk and three chairs were complemented by a magazine table "loaned by Mrs. Charley Wayland."

Though the initial plan had been to loan the books free-of-charge, it was decided that a membership fee of 25 cents a year be levied "if you could pay it," the reasoning being that "things paid for were of more value than those obtained for nothing." Dorothy Earp opened The Library of Crozet two days per week, and all patrons were welcomed warmly by Miss Dorothy and her young protégé. Tea and home-baked goods were served to each visitor.

The plainly appointed little room on The Square soon became a social center for the village. More volunteer hosts were enlisted and the library's hours were increased. Its Membership Book stated: "The library is open every Tuesday, Wednesday, Friday and Saturday afternoon, from 4:30 until 6." On Tuesdays, Miss Dorothy Earp was on hand. The Wednesday host was Mrs. Clark; Friday, Mrs. Sharrard; and Saturday's patrons were welcomed by Mrs. Robert Wayland.

The original Crozet Library Membership Book recorded library fee transactions and read like a "Who's Who" of early families of Crozet. [Image courtesy of the Woman's Club of Crozet]

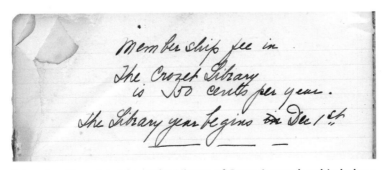

A hand-written detail from The Library of Crozet's membership ledger. The original library had a suggested annual subscription fee of 25 cents—raised to 50 cents after it reorganized and moved into the Crozet High School. [Image courtesy of the Woman's Club of Crozet.]

After a few years, readership declined as the hundred-or-so volumes in the library by then had been read by most, and no funds were available to purchase new books. It was decided to move the library's collection of books to the Crozet High School (then on Saint George Avenue) where some of its volumes helped to form the nucleus of the school library. Annual dues were increased to 50 cents, new books were purchased, and additional helpers came onboard to serve.

By 1915, general interest again had waned, and the books languished in a locked case at the school. The Crozet Free Library Association was formed with a goal of making the library's books available to all without charge. To qualify as a free library, the organization worked to raise the minimum $25 per year needed for the purchase of new books. In

Crozet's first library was on The Square in 1907. The storage room in which it was established (see arrow) was located next door to Crozet's combination Hotel-Hardware-Drug Store building.

November 1918, Crozet's first Free Library was founded.

John T. O'Neill offered the library free rent for a room next to his store building north of the depot, and a reading room was established there. The library grew and began a series of moves into various spaces around the village. From O'Neill's location it moved into a room over the Bank of Crozet on Main Street. From there, it went down the street to the Methodist Church until, in 1923, its collection of 524 books lovingly was taken over by the Woman's Club of Crozet. In 1928, the volumes were moved into the club's new home on the corner of Carter Street and Jarman's Gap Road.

At the Woman's Club location, an active and dedicated Library Committee contributed mightily to the growth and vitality of the library. By 1930, over 2600 volumes graced the bookshelves, and, in 1932, the "Dewey system of classification" was adopted.

During the height of the rigors on the home front while World War II raged, the library became inactive. Following the War's end, it was reopened, and a financial gift by the Crozet Lion's Club helped assure the library's continued operation. Near the end of that decade, Crozet's own library boasted nearly 3,000 titles.

The Woman's Club of Crozet was instrumental in securing for Albemarle County its first Bookmobile during the latter 1940s. This was a fortuitous investment because, for a season, the Bookmobile was the only library service available to the citizens of Crozet.

By 1963, Crozet's library needs had been served by the traveling bookmobile for ten years.

The activism of a citizen's committee representing 20 Crozet organizations led to the establishment of the Crozet Branch of the McIntire Public Library. In the spring of '64, the new Branch Library found quarters across the road from the train station in the former Chesley A. Haden & Co. office building.

Five years later, the Boy Scouts and others transported the library's inventory back to The Square, this time into the Crozet Hardware building. Interestingly, that building had been erected on the site of Dorothy Earp's first library endeavor.

When the hardware store returned to its previous location in the late 1970s, the library was forced to move back across the tracks yet again. Having grown in volumes-shelved and patrons-served, the library found very cramped quarters at a former location: the previous site of O'Neill's Store where the Crozet Free Library had opened its first reading room. Because of the difficulties created by downsizing and storage, the library's hours of operation—and corresponding visitor numbers—were greatly curtailed. The library languished in this state of limbo until 1984, when the philanthropic Perry Foundation rescued and renovated Crozet's abandoned C&O train station for the library's use.

For more than a quarter-century, Crozet has been served ably by a dedicated library staff in one of the town's most recognizable and historic structures. Has Crozet and western Albemarle County grown during that period? Like gangbusters! To continue to serve efficiently one of the

The Crozet Library was housed in the clubhouse of the Woman's Club for 25 years. The cataloged bookcases served as a backdrop for Cotillion dances, blood drives, well-baby clinics and numerous other public and private community functions. [Photo courtesy of the Woman's Club of Crozet.]

fastest growing areas in the county, Herculean demands have been placed on the staff in one of Jefferson-Madison Regional Library's busiest branches. A dearth of parking has added to the woes of visitors and employees alike.

It is now past time for the venerable Chesapeake and Ohio Railway depot to enter yet another realm of service to the Crozet community. The Crozet Library staff and the citizens of this region require a much larger and more technologically modern library facility. The hopes of securing public monies to meet this pressing need are dwindling.

Might the women who strived so diligently to keep the Crozet Library vital through our earlier days of war and economic peril have seen this present day approaching? Perhaps there was among them a mother with the foresight to sew some deep pockets into her child's clothing just for such a once-in-a-lifetime opportunity as this one. The blank pages of that future chapter of Crozet's library await a writer.

The Woman's Club of Crozet, established in 1920, assumed the responsibilities of the Crozet Library in 1923. The library was moved into their clubhouse following its construction in 1928. Volunteers from this community-minded organization administered the library for 30 years. [Photo courtesy of the Woman's Club of Crozet.]

Samuel Miller (1792–1869); son of old Albemarle County, Virginia; benevolent benefactor of Lynchburg Female Orphan Asylum and the Miller Manual Labor School of Albemarle.

21
Samuel Miller's School

Scientific American Magazine **published this engraved view of Miller School in 1886.**

What do you get if you take two barefoot country boys and send them on a scramble up a mountainside in search of ripe blackberries on a warm July day? The answer might surprise you.

John Miller and his younger brother Samuel were born and raised in a log cabin on a spur of the Ragged Mountains near Batesville, Virginia: poor boys living amongst an extended family of poor folks. Their earliest education was the hard labor associated with a subsistence lifestyle in the late 18th century. As much as their help was surely needed at home, their mother Jane made sure that they also attended the common school at Batesville whenever it was in session.

Resting together on the mountainside high above their cabin home, blackberry pails beside them, their casual conversations would have been typical of other youth their age living in similar conditions: bullies at school, rabbit traps, fishing holes, gathering some commodity from nature's storehouse to trade for a piece of candy at the mercantile in the village. One of the brothers could have ventured aloud what he might do if he were ever rich enough to have a whole dollar to spend on whatever he wanted, and each listened attentively as the other's wish-list was spoken. We will never know exactly how the subject arose, but one thing is sure: the boys agreed at an early age that if they could ever do anything to improve their poor mother's situation, they would. And then they would figure a way to help children like themselves have greater opportunities than the hardscrabble life they were living. Heady aspirations for barefoot boys, but the two young fellows were determined to stick to their guns.

Following the completion of his education in Batesville, John, the elder brother, headed south to Lynchburg, Virginia, where he found work as a merchant. Samuel, meanwhile, labored on, not only in his school work, but also picking up the slack at home created by the departure of his older brother. Samuel applied himself well enough in his studies that he "graduated" to teaching

CHESAPEAKE AND OHIO RAILWAY

"The Rhine, the Alps and the Battle-field Line"

ONLY ROUTE BETWEEN
THE MILLER MANUAL LABOR SCHOOL
Via Crozet, Virginia
——AND——
WASHINGTON, BALTIMORE, PHILADELPHIA, NEW YORK,
OLD POINT COMFORT, RICHMOND, NORFOLK, VIR-
GINIA HOT SPRINGS, CINCINNATI, LOUIS-
VILLE, INDIANAPOLIS, ST. LOUIS
CHICAGO.
INCOMPARABLE PANORAMA OF MOUNTAIN, RIVER AND CANON SCENERY
Wide Vestibule, Electric Lighted, Newly Equipped Trains
Observation and Pullman Cars—A'la Carte Dining Cars
STOP OVER ALLOWED AT WASHINGTON
For further information apply to nearest ticket agent or address,
H. W. FULLER, G. P. A., Washington, D. C.

Top image: Mailed from Miller School in 1910, this generic-style penny postcard was sent to Cousin Ida at Charlottesville's Woolen Mills community thanking her "for the nice Christmas present." *Bottom image:* Without Samuel Miller's school, the C&O Depot and eventual village known as Crozet, may never have come into existence. The former whistle-stop was outfitted to receive the vast quantities of materials required to construct and outfit the school—the grandest project of its kind in the south.

school at Batesville—a low-paying job that he kept until a better opportunity presented itself.

Better opportunity came knocking for Samuel Miller in an invitation to partner with his brother in Lynchburg. John's homegrown work ethic was paying off, and, together with Samuel, they grew their mercantile business and made shrewd investments with their increases.

The brothers, true to their earlier vow, made certain their mother's needs were met in their absence. They purchased farmland for her near their former cabin home and entrusted Batesville merchant Nicholas Murrell Page with its oversight. Page, through regular consultation with the brothers, saw to it that the property was kept in good order and that Jane's needs were met. This working relationship, based on mutual trust, would eventually pay even grander dividends.

Samuel Miller's world changed forever in 1841 following the death of his mother, and the passing of his brother John, his lifelong friend and business partner. Jane was buried close by the home her sons had provided for her.

John Miller's will bequeathed all of his assets, valued at nearly $100,000—a veritable fortune in its day—to his younger brother. The dreams the two brothers had originally shared in the Ragged Mountains would become a defining goal for Samuel Miller as he stood poised in the prime of his days.

Moving outside of Lynchburg while still maintaining an interest in his mercantile, Samuel Miller lived a mostly private life. He invested his monies in overseas markets and a wisely diversified assortment of bonds.

In 1859, he drew up a detailed will, which revealed at his death in 1869 not only a fortune greatly exceeding one million dollars, but also his varied benevolent leanings. Of the three executors named in Miller's will, only his trusted friend, Batesville merchant Nicholas Page, had survived him.

With extraordinary integrity and tenacity, Page entered into the work of putting into order Miller's papers and estate. Hiring wise and experienced counsel, he met and overcame numerous challenges from various heirs of the estate, finishing the trying work by insuring that the great majority of Miller's bequests were implemented successfully.

Miller's philanthropy led to his becoming known as one of Virginia's greatest benefactors; the vast majority of Samuel Miller's estate went toward education. The University of Virginia received what was, at that time, one of its largest gifts. The Lynchburg Female Orphan Asylum had been established by Miller prior to his death, and his final directives assured its future. He was buried there on its grounds.

His most visible legacy, however, was the establishment of the Miller Manual Labor School of Albemarle, "a School on the Manual-Labor principle … there shall be fed, clothed, and instructed in all the branches of a good, plain, sound English education, the various languages, both ancient and modern, agriculture, and the useful arts, and wholly free of expense to the pupils, as many poor orphan children, and other white children whose parents are unable to educate them…"

Culminating an amazing two years of construction, the school opened for business in the fall of 1878 under the direction of its first Superintendent, Prof. Charles E. Vawter. Just as through Miller's wise selection of Nicholas Page as his executor the school became a possibility, Vawter's election by the school's governing board made possible a solid foundation for the school's success and future. C.E. Vawter led the school for 27 years and died there, as he had wished, "in harness."

Today, 130 years later, The Miller School of Albemarle stands tall on an international stage, its 21st century feet firmly planted on a solid foundation. Successive years of exemplary leadership

Captain Charles Erastus Vawter, first Superintendent of Miller Manual Labor School, is pictured surrounded by Miller's 1904 football team. [Courtesy of Steve Craig]

have continued to mold John and Samuel Miller's dream of "maximizing the potential" of young people.

A tribute was written more than a century ago and published in Volume One of the Miller School class yearbook, *The Blue Ridge Blast*. It is no less fitting these many decades later.

> To Samuel Miller
> founder of the Miller School
> who, when an abjectly poor boy, formed the
> unvarying purpose of his life, to build a school
> where, with abundant means and rare educational
> facilities, the special objects of his care could
> through all time have opportunity, hope and life,
> This First Volume
> is most lovingly dedicated by those, now
> grown to be men and women, whom
> his generous forethought blessed
> and sent into the world
> to help others and to
> do honor to his memory.

Girls were first enrolled in Miller Manual beginning in 1884. Though their housing and classes were kept separate, a co-ed campus certainly made day-to-day life more interesting.

22
Old Afton Village

The earlier Afton Depot and passenger walkway were elevated to be on level with the raised rail bed. An enlarged replacement tunnel, bored in 1943-44, was placed at a lower grade.

Hoppin' might be one word to describe the village of Afton a century ago.

Claudius Crozet didn't originate the phrase, "If you build it, they will come," but that adage was proven over and again wherever railroading designated a regular stopping point for its trains. A year after the first steam train passed through the Blue Ridge Tunnel in 1858, the village of Afton opened for business with the appointments of a depot and post office.

In earlier years, the hardy travelers who had navigated the winding trail traversing the steep, northernmost tip of Nelson County below Rockfish Gap would have made little note of the future site of Afton. Then-Governor Thomas Jefferson and the Virginia General Assembly surely didn't pause there for cookies when they fled westward in 1781 to avoid capture by Tarleton's British Dragoons. Neither was there yet anything to draw attention to the place when Jefferson and Madison passed through on horseback 37 years later to meet with other dignitaries at the Rockfish Gap Tavern to decide the location of *Central College*, today's University of Virginia.

Civil Engineer Crozet surely noted, though, in 1838, where his survey line crossed the Staunton and Scottsville Turnpike as he planned for a potential rail passage westward through the Blue Ridge Mountains. Just over ten years later, the work commenced, and the future site of the village of Afton became a staging area for materials for his ambitious project. Clusters of laborers' shanties offered the first hint of the bustling village to come.

The lyrical words of the Scottish Bard Robert Burns in his poem *Sweet Afton* inspired the

Afton Chapel was built in 1898 and continues to serve its community. It sits just downhill from the site of the original Afton House hotel.

naming of several towns in America: "How lofty, sweet Afton, thy neighboring hills,/ Far mark'd with the courses of clear winding rills…/ How pleasant thy banks and green valleys below,/ Where, wild in the woodlands, the primroses blow."

That idyllic scene, well-describing this village in Virginia's Blue Ridge Mountains, was marred throughout the Civil War years when both Confederate and Union forces overwhelmed the mountain community, leaving its little depot in ashes and steel rails brutally bent.

Soon following this destruction, however, life settled into its new normal. In 1867, a merchant named Pugh at Afton Depot put out the following notice: "I shall constantly keep on hand or furnish on Short Notice fine groceries and Plaster which I will sell cheap for Cash or exchange for Produce such as Corn, wheat, Rye Oats & Bacon at Richmond prices, expenses deducted. I also keep on hand the Celebrated Livingston Plow and Castings of all the different numbers."

In 1869, Afton moved from being only a shipping and receiving point to becoming a travel destination. Afton House, an imposing four-story summer resort, was established and presided over by James Goodloe for more than 50 years. Sited with a grand view of the celebrated Rockfish Valley, its welcome breezes and gracious accommodations were especially popular among those from Richmond and the Tidewater lowlands. Guests arriving on the C&O trains had only a short stroll from the railroad depot to where they could relax on its broad porches and wait for the call to the dining room.

England's Queen Victoria had kindled a local industry soon after her coronation in 1838, with her penchant for the Albemarle Pippin. The Queen's apple was especially suitable for growth along the mountainous slopes in the region. With the coming of the railroad, more fruit producers sprang up to take advantage of the convenient shipping. The seasonal bonanza proved a boon to Afton's bottom line, providing even more opportunities for employment.

By the turn of the 20th-century the village of Afton was self-supporting and getting along just fine, thank you. Local residents were working as coopers providing barrels to orchardists, support staff at the hotel, several general merchants, blacksmiths and those performing repair work, all in addition to orchard and farm work, and a variety of railroad jobs.

Afton's horizon continued to shine brightly for many decades. Two distinctive mountaintop

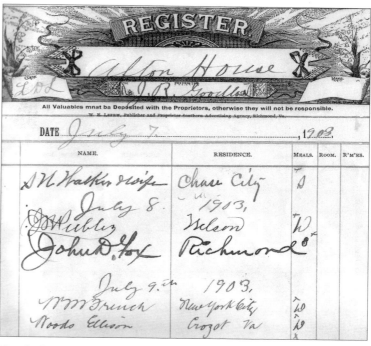

The desk register of the Afton House in 1903 recorded local travelers along with train passengers who stopped for meals and lodging. [Courtesy of the Edward S. Stratton family.]

mansions were built nearby. All of the automobile and truck traffic traveling across the mountain continued to pass through the village for the next 40+ years, and service stations and garages were established to accommodate the traveling public's needs.

Orchardists once converged at Afton to ship their fruit via the Chesapeake and Ohio Railway.

The original Afton House was a summer resort built by James R. Goodloe in 1869. It was destroyed by fire in 1963.

Beginning in 1976, the squealing of bicycles braking because of the enticing aroma of fresh-baked cookies wafting from the home next door to Haven's Garage would replace the once-welcomed sounds of commerce that formerly had arrived multiple times a day at the nearby train station. E. S. Stratton's Antique Shop next door to the Post Office would parcel out the few remaining remnants of the former mountain resort town's storied past before it, too, faded into history.

Sweet Afton holds dear its sweet memories of the hustle and bustle of another time and the sojourners who added so much life to its days.

Old Mr. Jefferson and his companions never knew the commotion they had missed.

A view of Afton, Virginia, at the turn of the 20th- century. A few more buildings were constructed later to service the auto traveler. [Courtesy of the Library of Congress, Prints & Photographs Division.]

23

Back Home in Jarman's Gap

Two descendants of the Jarman family enjoy a cool drink of water from the ancestral spring during their visit with Anna Rogers. Mountaintop pastures were common prior to the establishment of Shenandoah National Park. [Photo courtesy of Purcell and Dorothy Mowry Daughtry.]

When Gertrude Rogers Simms left Jarman's Gap in the 1950s on her first visit to Washington, D.C., she got to experience firsthand how the other half lived—and she didn't like all of what she heard and saw.

"My Aunt Cora Lee took me up there to stay with her for a while," Gertrude recalled. "The houses were so close together—and I never heard so many whistles [sirens]. I wouldn't drive in that place for nothing."

Gertrude's aunt, who lived on Pennsylvania Avenue, left home early in the morning to go to work at the Pentagon. Gertrude stayed alone the rest of the day, trying to sort out a new world of strange sounds and constant activity. Two weeks later she was back home.

"When they brought me back, I told Aunt Cora Lee—we were coming up the road here 'cause we lived up in the hollow then—'I'm going to get out and kiss this ground.' I was back home! No, I just don't care for the city."

Not many among us can recall the transition of these mountains from working farmlands dotted with homesteads to forested park land with limited access. Gertrude Simms knew the former

This railroad sign once served as a reference point for train engineers where the C&O's tracks crossed Jarman's Gap Road. It was photographed by Jarman family descendant Sam P. Clarke in the early 1970's.

days when Jarman's Gap Road gave unrestricted access across the mountaintop and down into the valley. During a span of 200 years, Jarman's Gap experienced every form of traveler and conveyance.

Michael Woods, an Irish immigrant, led his family south from Pennsylvania along the Great Valley Road in 1734. In Augusta County he turned east and crossed "The Blue Ledge" into present day western Albemarle County. The ancient footpath they followed eastward across the Blue Ridge Mountains would become a key feature in Virginia's early road system. Woods and his family entourage, which included his son-in-law, William Wallace, diligently set about to establish themselves in the fertile Piedmont. Woods acquired over 3,300 acres of land extending from the mountaintop gap that bore his name to the bottom lands along Lickinghole Creek and Mechum's River. He named his sprawling estate "Mountain Plains," and by 1737 established a house of worship where his family could exercise their devout Presbyterian faith. The Mountain Plain Baptist Church near Mechum's River perpetuates that name to this day.

Woods was authorized in 1737 "to Clear a road from the Blew Ledge of Mountains down to Ivy Creek." Improvement of the primitive foot and bridle path allowed passage by wheeled vehicles and advanced the route that came to be known as Three Notch'd Road. It helped to open a trade route between agricultural interests in the Shenandoah Valley and the expanding political and economic opportunities in Richmond.

In 1780 and 1781, Hessian prisoners who had been incarcerated at The Barracks near Charlottesville during the

The Jarman's Gap community once supported two different churches. The former church building pictured here in lower Jarman's Gap had an active congregation in the early decades of the twentieth century, but more recently served as a private residence. Henry Rogers dragged the logs that were used to build the church that once stood in upper Jarman's Gap.

Revolutionary War were marched through Woods Gap. In a letter written following their mountain passage, a British officer stated that, although the Blue Mountains were loftier than the mountains they crossed in Connecticut, the crossing at Woods Gap was much easier "owing to the judicious manner that the inhabitants had made the road, which by its winding renders the ascent extremely easy." In 1781, the Augusta Militia met at Woods Gap and marched to Richmond in response to reports that the British were heading west.

By 1788, John Blair, Jr. had taken possession of Mountain Plains, and since then it has been known as Blair Park. Blair, a legal scholar from Williamsburg, was nominated by George Washington as one of the original members of the United States Supreme Court.

Henry Rogers relaxes with his mother, Anna, beside her home in Jarman's Gap. [Photo courtesy of Gertrude Rogers Simms.]

Thomas Jarman purchased lands at the summit of Woods Gap around 1790, built a log house there and planted tobacco. The gap came to be identified with him and is known today as Jarman's Gap. As Jarman prospered, he added on to the house and purchased additional slaves to care for his holdings.

In 1827, a slave named Julie was born on Jarman's plantation. From her home near the mountaintop, Julie was witness to countless Civil War maneuvers that eventually culminated in her freedom. In 1862, following a successful Valley Campaign, part of Stonewall Jackson's army moved through Jarman's Gap en route to Richmond to bolster Confederate General Robert E. Lee. Jackson's mapmaker, Jed Hotchkiss, often found shelter and passage in Jarman's Gap. Following a skirmish in the Valley on March 1, 1865, Union General Philip Sheridan eluded Confederate pursuers by slipping through Jarman's Gap. The following day his forces captured Charlottesville. A little over one month later, four years of conflict ended with the final surrender at Appomatox.

Following the war, Thomas Jarman told his former slaves that they and their families could remain on the property if they so chose. Among those who stayed were Julie and her family, who adopted the surname Rogers. As the war was drawing to a close, Julie Rogers gave birth to a daughter whom she named Anna.

Anna Rogers lived her entire life in Jarman's Gap, eventually moving into the old Jarman homeplace. She has been remembered as a meticulous homemaker and gracious hostess to her visitors. In addition to raising a garden, she hunted wild game on the mountainside. Prior to the forming of Shenandoah National Park, absentee landowners harvested the timber and established grazing lands for their livestock along the Blue Ridge mountaintops. Local mountain dwellers were hired to care for the livestock. Anna also performed that service for a Valley family during the early decades of the twentieth century.

Anna bore only one son, Henry Rogers. Henry's daughter, Gertrude, fondly recalls living "up in the hollow" near her grandmother.

"We were the only colored people that lived up on Jarman Gap. That was the Rogers. Now I'm the only colored woman on Jarman—all the rest of 'em done died and left here, but I'm still hanging in here by the help of God. I know He's taken care of me, 'cause if it hadn't been for Him, I don't know where I'd have been."

Gertrude Simms' days are filled with activity. Neighbors and family members regularly call or stop in. And she has a list of others with whom she makes regular telephone contact. She enjoys a true contentment—the pleasing, mature fruit of a life of hard work, staying close to her roots, and taking a genuine interest in the people who cross her path.

"I like this mountain," Gertrude said, as she reflected on her life in Jarman's Gap. "Well, maybe it's 'cause I'm a old country woman. I'm stuck up here on this little hill, all these bushes and things. And my barking dog. And I *am* happy!"

The former Thomas Jarman house as it appeared in 1941 during the latter years that Anna Rogers lived there. [Photo courtesy of Purcell and Dorothy Mowry Daughtry.]

24

Killer Tornado—1959!

Mountain Plain Baptist Church at Mechum's River, sustained extensive damage in 1959 from a tornado spawned from remnants of Hurricane Gracie. [Photo courtesy of Les Gibson, Crozet.]

Leana Simms was at work preparing supper for W. E. Lindsay's household near the village of Ivy when she became witness to one of Albemarle County's most horrific natural disasters. When a dark swirling cloud descended into her neighborhood, her thoughts quickly turned to the well-being of her neighbors. A year later she could still clearly replay the awful scene in her mind.

"I went down there," Mrs. Simms told a Charlottesville *Daily Progress* reporter, "and I found death and destruction."

During the afternoon of Wednesday, September 30, 1959, at least seven tornados spun devastation across central Virginia in a span of about three hours. In the twisters' paths, 12 souls, adults and children, had their final breath snatched away. The indiscriminate winds left many others homeless and hurting. Houses and barns, cars and trucks, personal belongings—the *things* of life—were strewn about, as one harrowed survivor recalled, "like a piece of tissue paper."

Hurricane Gracie had meandered erratically in the Atlantic for five days before coming ashore south of Charleston, South Carolina. Its lethal combination of wind, rain and flooding claimed ten lives in that state. As it progressed through the Carolinas into southwest Virginia, it became

Little remained of the home of Ervin Morris Sr. near Ivy, where ten members of one family perished in a tornado in September 1959. [Photo courtesy of Les Gibson.]

noted as well for the beneficial rains which the accompanying thunderstorms produced.

Few took particular note when, around 2:25 p.m., telephone and electrical service were lost to much of western Albemarle County. After all, there were thunderstorms in the area, and such a temporary inconvenience was not unheard-of. There was no way of knowing at the time that the outage was the result of tornado #1 that had downed trees, power and phone lines northwest of Ivy Depot before vanishing over open ground.

Around 4:15 p.m. several witnesses detected in the cloudy, rainy skies a "black funnel" forming south of Charlottesville. Crossing Rt. 29, tornado #2, a killer by nature, began its destructive traverse by overturning a car. Passing over Ragged Mountain, it veered northwest, "plowed a furrow 200 feet wide over a sharp ridge" and dropped down into a small valley on Lindsay's farm near Ivy.

"I had watched it come in," said Leana Simms, "but I didn't know what it was. It was inky black above and snow white below, like a black cloud swirling around. It sounded like a lot of airplanes. Then I couldn't look to see what was going on—part of the roof blew off… I thought of all those people down there in those houses, and I thought maybe I should go to see about them."

Nearby, Raymond Bruce with his wife and son were already scrambling for their lives.

"I heard a roaring up the back orchard," Bruce later told a reporter. "It sounded like a train. I saw Ervin Morris running into his house, and then the roof started coming off my house. The roof went up about 50 yards."

The 14-member Morris family lived a hundred yards away from the Bruces in a two-story duplex. Twelve members of the family were already home and preparing for supper when the deadly winds took direct aim at their dwelling. It would be over two hours before the outside world began to piece together the events that unfolded.

As the twister lifted the roof from the Bruce home, the family ran to the kitchen. At that moment the chimney collapsed, killing Lilly Bruce while only slightly injuring her husband and son.

An instant later the tornado's full fury swept away the Morris dwelling, scattering its occupants and their belongings hundreds of yards about the surrounding hillsides.

Leana Simms crawled over and through splintered trees to make her way to the storm's ground-zero. She paused to wrap Mrs. Bruce's lifeless body in a blanket and, further along, did the same for Mrs. Morris and two of her children.

"I could hear children crying," Simms vividly recalled. With help she was able to extract a little girl pinned under part of a bed tangled in the debris. When rescue personnel finally made their way over flooded, tree-strewn roads, it took them most of the night to locate the other victims. The last one found, a young child, was located with the aid of the next morning's light. The vicious onslaught had taken ten family members; only two miraculously survived. Two of the family's other children were unharmed as they had waited out the after-school deluge at a neighbor's house.

At John Clayton's farm the twister destroyed barns and returned 7,000 bales of hay to the fields to be gathered and baled a second time. [Photo courtesy of Les Gibson.]

This row of trucks belonging to John W. Clayton and Son was unscathed during the tornado that destroyed many buildings around them—including the garage shelter under which they had been parked. [Photo courtesy of Les Gibson.]

Short minutes later the Mechum's River community lay in the storm's path. Twisting and turning, the storm's forces collapsed the front wall of Mountain Plain Baptist Church, carrying away part of the roof and laying bare the sanctuary to its rains.

Racing back down the hill, the fury spun across Mechum's River's steel C&O railroad trestle, simultaneously blasting away at Rt. 250 below with an arsenal of projectiles. Staunton residents Glenn Womble and his wife Josephine unwittingly drove directly into the center of the storm. They sought refuge alongside the embankment under the railroad bridge. Approaching from the west, the driver of a heavy truck, which had been tipping side-to-side in the winds, stopped and also sought some degree of cover against the embankment.

"All around us timbers, tin, signs, trees, paper, gravel [and] sand were flying," Mrs. Womble told a *Staunton Leader* reporter. "We thought our car would be lifted any moment and thrown into the river... pieces of wood and rock smashed our windshield... we felt that the bridge was being destroyed and falling upon us... we expected to be crushed to death any second... wind lifted the truck right up and it was thrown [a full 50 yards] in front of our car."

The tornado then retraced its path back up Old Three Notch'd Road and laid great waste to the farm of John W. Clayton. The roof was lifted from his main house which was damaged beyond repair—all while Mrs. Martha Clayton remained at her work desk. (Several days later O.B. Enswiler of Lacey Springs, Virginia, personally returned to the thankful Clayton family a water-stained paid-up bank note. He had found it in his yard—50 miles northwest across the Blue

Ridge Mountains—deposited there by the winds that had plucked it from atop Mrs. Clayton's desk.)

The twelfth fatality in Central Virginia occurred just north of the Albemarle-Greene County line near Dyke. Blue Ridge School was hard-hit by possibly the same killer storm that had just devastated Ivy and Mechum's River. Students at the boarding school were spared injury, but school maintenance worker Robert Morris was critically hurt when an equipment shed collapsed on him. He died later from his storm-inflicted injuries.

Between 4:45 and 5:30 P.M. at least five other tornados touched down in Albemarle County. In the Hickory Hill area south of Charlottesville, a miraculous outcome resulted when another home containing 12 persons was totally demolished by tornado #3, injuring only one. Yards away, a tractor trailer and two autos were tossed from busy Rt. 29. Trees and outbuildings were destroyed by twin tornados in Stoney Point. Around 5:25 yet another twister damaged homes near the University Airport east of Monticello Mountain. The last known tornado in Albemarle that day inflicted heavy damage on several homes and trees in the Farmington neighborhood.

Following the cessation of the storms, local roads began to fill with sightseers rubber-necking for a glimpse of nature's devastation. More importantly, though, were the hundreds of benevolent hands that converged where their help was severely needed. For weeks and months they returned until the clean-up and repairs were complete.

Three days later 500 people attended the emotion-filled mass funeral for the Morris family of

This house had sheltered Raymond Bruce, his wife and son until it was devastated by a twister spawned by once-Hurricane Gracie. When the tempest lifted the roof from the home, Mrs. Bruce died when she was crushed by the subsequent chimney collapse. [Photo courtesy of Les Gibson.]

On Clayton's hilltop farm near Mechum's River, numerous barns and work sheds were lost. The main house was damaged beyond repair. Fences were blown flat to the ground releasing livestock. And, amazingly, a water pump with twenty-odd feet of pipe still attached was sucked from a well. [Photo courtesy of Les Gibson.]

Ivy. Buried side-by-side at Hebron Baptist Church at Avon in Nelson County were: "Ervin Morris Sr., and his wife Frances; their children, Ruby and James; Mrs. Ervin Morris Jr., and her two children, Peggy and Michael; George Morris, brother of Ervin Sr., and Wilmer Morris, nephew of Ervin Sr."

We are especially reminded of the temporal worth of *things* and the eternal value of human *relationships* during tragedies such as these. The selfless motives of neighbors like Leana Simms and other nameless volunteers serve as examples of the grace we might all hope to emulate should we suddenly be called upon.

25

Acme Visible Records

The Tool and Die department at Acme was one of a full complement of manufacturing capabilities. New product ideas brought through the front door were designed and produced in-house at Crozet. [Acme Visible Voice image courtesy of Shirley McCauley Cook.]

Who, after working alongside someone for any length of time, does not feel a personal connection that transcends the task at hand? When those jobs endure for years, and relationships intertwine through mealtimes and the casual sharing of joys and hardships, community is born. One such working community began in Crozet, Virginia, in 1949.

K. K. Knickerbocker's Acme Visible Records, originally founded as the Acme Card System Company, had been manufacturing office record-keeping equipment and supplies since 1914. During World War II his Chicago, Illinois, plant (and many other manufacturing plants across the country) was temporarily converted to the production of products needed for the war effort. Following the war's end, however, demand for Acme's office products increased almost beyond the Chicago facility's ability to produce them.

George Anderson had followed in his father's footsteps when he joined Acme Card System's Chicago workforce as an errand boy. By the time the company's name changed to Acme Visible Records, Inc., in 1937, Anderson's ten years of service were rewarded with promotion to Factory Office Manager. He remembered Acme's post-war boom this way: "Prior to 1950 manufacturing was located in an old multiple-story building of 50,000 square feet in Chicago. Not only was the building congested, but much machinery was obsolete. Shipping worked around the clock in order to clear space for the next day's production."

During a visit with a friend in Albemarle County, Knickerbocker determined the sure advantages of relocating his company, and, in 1949, Acme Visible purchased the first of several tracts of land that would become its Crozet worldwide headquarters.

The ACME Way
ALL CARDS IN SIGHT

A SINGLE MOVE FINDS ANY CARD

Construction of the initial plant facility began soon thereafter, and when the transplanted company's first local hires reported to work in mid-1950, "the floor wasn't finished in the new factory, and dump trucks were inside pouring gravel." These pioneer employees assisted in unloading boxcars of machinery, equipment and supplies shipped down from Chicago, and setting up the plant as the new floors cured.

The rural neighborhood where the new Acme plant was located had seen its fair share of activity during the hundred years since Claudius Crozet's work crews had excavated and built the railroad berm that defined the region. Well-cultivated farms and orchards fronted the highway east of Crozet. Acme's land holdings came to encompass several of those farmsteads worked by local families such as Ballard, Gibson, Graves, Henley, Morris, Sandridge, Thurston and others.

Passers-by not many years earlier might have seen Tom Hicks working his cornfield, and his granddaughter Ruby scampering across the road to carry him a cool drink of water. Or they might have spied the Gypsy camp that would occasionally set-up just down the road. Others might have stopped for gasoline or repair work at one of the (*five!*) service stations between Crozet and Mechum's River Depot. During peach season, C.C. Wade's fruit packing shed, originally built by Loyd Gibson directly behind his service station, was a beehive of activity with wagons and truckloads of fruit arriving while boxcars waited on the shed's rail siding.

The Gibson family homeplace once stood on the property where the new Acme facility was built. Gibson's Service Station, closed since its owner's death in 1933, was removed during Acme's property renovations, but the adjacent fruit packing shed was adapted for use as the company's maintenance facility. The former Ballard house was occupied by the Acme Visible Records Federal Credit Union.

A house does not necessarily make a home; neither does a manufacturing facility incubate a community. But each of these places can shelter and nurture families and communities when their inhabitants agree to work together genuinely. Acme was populated with workers from Crozet and Albemarle County, and surrounding counties. Employees relied on one another for rides to work, and for instruction and aid on the job. They also enjoyed spending leisure time together during

In 1920, Acme Visible's predecessor, the Acme Card System Co. of Chicago, Illinois, advertised internationally in Systems **magazine. [Acme Visible Voice image courtesy of Shirley McCauley Cook.]**

Loyd and Florence Gibson operated Gibson's Service Station and garage on Crozet's east side in the 1920s and '30s. The placement of Acme's main entrance in 1950 necessitated the station's removal. The grove of trees to the right is where Musictoday and Starr Hill Brewing Co. are now located. [Photo courtesy of Les Gibson.]

Visitors entering the Acme Visible plant at Crozet were treated to a display of the company's newest products. In the early 1970s the Stratomatic power filing system (pictured here) complemented other Acme products which carried futuristic names such as Astromatic and Centrac. [Acme Visible Voice image courtesy of Shirley McCauley Cook.]

Acme Visible sponsored a baseball team during its very first year of operation. Ballplayers on that early team often recalled competing against future Major League Baseball Hall-of-Famer Willie Mays during the State Semi-Pro Tournament in 1952. Mays had played with the New York Giants in 1951, but was drafted into the U.S. Army in 1952. He participated in the Charlottesville tournament while playing for the Fort Eustis baseball team. [Photo courtesy of Alvin Toms.]

their evenings and weekends.

The employee-run Social Activities Club sponsored and promoted opportunities for sports, recreation and travel. In early days employee picnics were held on company property in "Acme Grove." As the activities club grew, many employees participated on numerous company sports teams. SAC-sponsored bus trips carried groups of co-workers and their families to special events and destinations far and wide.

Everyone—over 1,000 employees locally and in regional offices—was kept informed and "on the same page" by the employee-published newspaper, the *Acme Visible Voice*. Within months of the plant's opening, every manner of management and employee celebration and concern was being shared through the pages of the Visible Voice: from company contracts and housekeeping reminders, to anniversaries, sports results and personal items for sale. And photos—*always* lots of employee photos.

In 1975, Acme's growing printing department moved out of Crozet and into a new facility in Louisa County. Production continued strongly, but within a decade, corporate mergers and buy-outs brought changes. By the time all of the name changes played out—American Brands, Kwik-File, Acme Design Technology, Mayline, Wilson-Jones—the loyal, consistent co-workers of

Acme Visible Records was the first major industry to locate in Crozet. This late-1950s view shows a plant expansion under way. The facility's front lawn still contained the remnant of a fruit orchard, and farm land across the highway remained under cultivation. [Photo by Mac Sandridge.]

Knickerbocker's Acme Visible had been dispersed.

George Anderson—with 50 years of Acme service—spoke highly of management's admiration of Acme's workforce. In 1971 he wrote, "We enjoy the benefits of the modern manufacturing facility of approx. 220,000 sq. ft., well lighted, air conditioned and equipped with up-to-date machines. Foremost, however, our management can enjoy and appreciate one of the most productive and conscientious work forces in industry today. This workforce takes pride in all job assignments and is dedicated to high productivity... quality [and] craftsmanship."

Likewise, longtime Acme employee Lucille Bruce, regarded by many as poet laureate of Acme and beloved for her verses of regional interest, wrote in 1976 from the Acme employee's perspective:

Pioneer Association

In the heart of the Blue Ridge Mountains
Surrounded by skies of blue
Where pages of history lay written
There's a page for Acme, too.
Stately standing by the busy highway
Where the wheels of progress grind.
We've each been a part of her heartbeat
As her strength and growth unwind.
Like pioneers at the beginning
We numbered only a few.
Faithfully we kept going onward
As Acme steadily grew.
Our lives are entwined with Acme
While we give of ourselves each day

To the jobs that have been assigned us
And the friends that we've made by the way.
We've had our good times and bad ones
Oft' times midst laughter or tears
Acme to us has been a by-word
For its faithful Pioneers.
Many faces are no longer with us
The new ones come and go
But those who have faithfully lingered
Have seen the "Infant Acme" grow.
We are proud of the progress of Acme
Her products are known thru the land.
It gives us a wonderful feeling
That we are part of her "Pioneer Clan."

Moletus and Sarah (Frazier) Garrison with their children at their home on the crest of the Blue Ridge Mountains in Albemarle County. Like many others, the Garrison family was forced off their land for the creation of Shenandoah National Park. [Photo courtesy of Woodrow and Rosie Keyton.]

26

Shenandoah National Park: The Hidden Sacrifice

Robert H. "Bob" Via sits with two youngsters in the midst of baskets and barrels of Albemarle Pippin apples. Bob Via unsuccessfully challenged the Commonwealth of Virginia's right to take his Blue Ridge Mountain land and orchards and give them to the federal government. [Photo courtesy of Leon Via III.]

President Franklin Roosevelt dedicated Shenandoah National Park on the 3rd of July 1936, "to this and succeeding generations of Americans for the recreation and for the *re*-creation which they shall find here." Ten years of struggle, great sacrifice, and countless tears had preceded this speech expounding on land conservation and the motorized pursuit of happiness by the American people.

Now, imagine living in a place where everything you need for work and play is available just a short distance from your front door. Throw in spectacular views, a network of roads with only occasional traffic, and good neighbors whose ancestral roots run as deeply in that place as your own.

Then, imagine that when your children reach adulthood and are continuing the same traditions which were handed down to you, a law is established that requires them to abandon their homes, property, neighborhood and way of life.

Such was the case of Christopher Columbus Via, born the fourth of 13 siblings, and raised in the Blue Ridge Mountains of Albemarle County.

When Christopher Via was born in 1850, an agricultural census that same year noted that his grandfather Clifton Via was blessed to own a farmstead of several hundred acres and a wide variety of livestock. His field crops included oats, wheat, corn and tobacco while his gardens produced beans, potatoes and peas and other edible staples. Clifton Via's forefathers had farmed Albemarle County lands since the mid-1700's.

A traditionally strong work ethic led Christopher Columbus Via to establish an orchard of Albemarle Pippin apples in a 2,700' elevation wind gap below the crest of the Blue Ridge Mountains. His most select fruits were shipped to England, beginning that long trek from Via Gap by horse-and-wagon over the mountain to a railroad shipping point in the Shenandoah Valley. The balance of the crop was distilled into brandy for legal sale. The seasonal apple business supplemented his usual farming and timbering operations.

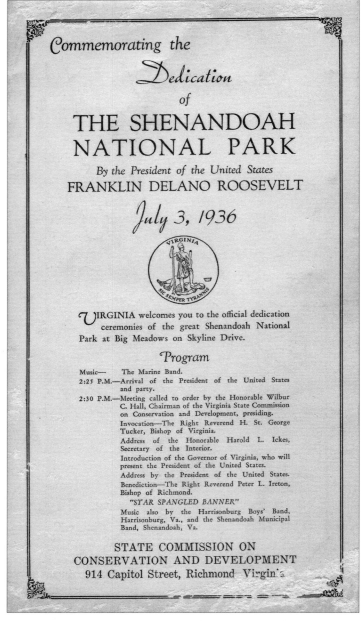

President Franklin D. Roosevelt officially dedicated Shenandoah National Park on July 3, 1936.

Via's commercial pursuits provided work for many in his neighborhood, and served as lessons in business for the fifteen children born to him and his wife Melinda (Marshall) Via. His hard-earned prosperity allowed him to contribute land for two community buildings: Wayside Brethren Church (built near the intersection of the North Fork of Moorman's River and Black Rock Gap Road), and Via School (built in the mountains alongside this same fork of the Moorman's River).

As America prospered and grew, forward-looking individuals began to call for the setting aside and conservation of certain public lands. The first such project was Yellowstone National Park, established in 1872. By the early 1920s more than a dozen U.S. National Parks had been established, all but one being in the western states. Post-World War prosperity coupled with mass-produced, affordable automobiles enabled Americans of modest means to become increasingly mobile.

A demand was raised to establish a national park easily accessed by the masses living in the eastern U.S. Much lobbying was done by states hoping to be awarded the unique distinction—and the tourism dollars—that such a designation would bring. In 1924 the Southern Appalachian National Park Committee recommended two sites: Great Smoky Mountains National Park in North Carolina/Tennessee and Shenandoah National Park in Virginia. In 1926 both parks were authorized by Congress—with the condition that their lands be donated.

The lands comprising Shenandoah National Park lie in eight Virginia counties. Congress had stipulated that the proposed park must contain a minimum of 160,000 acres. From 1926–1928 an area of more than 300,000 acres was surveyed for possible inclusion in the park. This included 344 individual tracts of land in Albemarle County totaling nearly 25,000 acres. Houses and barns were inspected, fruit trees were counted and values were placed on saleable timber. The Hoover administration had been willing to allow the mountain people to remain in their homes. The powers-that-be in Roosevelt's administration dashed the hopes of many when they decreed that all

Daniel C. Via (1877–1930) sitting on right, rests beside his sons, Jessie and Junie. Daniel followed the logging traditions of his father, Christopher Columbus Via, in the Via Gap area of western Albemarle. [Photo courtesy of Leon Via III.]

park inhabitants would have to move out.

Following a blanket condemnation by the state, monetary settlements were offered to titled land owners, and an appeals process (usually fruitless) began. Some owners were ready and willing to sell—many more were less than willing at the prices offered. Others were unwilling to sell or leave at any price.

Unease was the order of the day in many mountain settlements. Neighborhood meetings were held among the mountain dwellers, and correspondence, news and rumors were passed along. As individual appeals wore on and fears of the inevitable became more of a reality, landowners' letters to park and government authorities took on a different tone. Owners asked if they could move buildings, or requested permission to plant gardens or repair fences one more season. Individuals outside of the proposed park area asked to salvage materials from abandoned homes. Most citizen requests were denied.

Former renters and tenants of sold properties, having no legal or financial recourse in the condemnations, sometimes quietly moved into nearby recently abandoned houses. When discovered, they again were forced to

Joseph F. Wood (1871–1944) was the only Albemarle County landowner granted lifetime tenure following the establishment of Shenandoah National Park. He and his wife Winkie (Belew) raised their family on the south fork of Moorman's River in Sugar Hollow, near today's popular Blue Hole. [Photo courtesy of Larry Lamb.]

leave, and the houses were dismantled or burned to prevent repeat occurrences.

When it appeared to the remaining mountain residents that all recourse had been exhausted, a spark of hope was rekindled late in 1934. Albemarle County landowner Robert H. "Bob" Via (1883–1958), a son of Christopher Columbus Via, contended that "the state had no power to condemn property within the state for the purpose of making a gift of it to the United States." Via took his challenge against the State of Virginia to the federal courts.

Bob Via had no small interest in the state's condemnation affairs. He had continued his father's legacy in the Via Gap area by planting thousands more Albemarle Pippin trees, and netted $2000 annually (a princely sum in that day) on fruit sales alone. Though the federal court considered Via's arguments, his challenge died in November 1935 when the U.S. Supreme Court rejected

The gravestone of Christopher Columbus Via (1850–1906) and his wife Melinda (1849–1921) stands tall over the graves of their extended family members in the Via Cemetery. The National Park land condemnation took Via's former home with much of his mountain farm, and isolated the cemetery on private property.

his final appeal. A month later, on the day after Christmas 1935, over 176,000 acres of Virginia mountain lands were deeded to the federal government.

Thousands of park boosters were in attendance when President Roosevelt's dedicatory speech was presented in the grassy field at Big Meadows in Shenandoah National Park. Their appreciative applause echoed down the mountainsides, but few remained in the hollows and coves to wonder what the commotion was all about. The previous ten years, overseen by three presidential administrations, had been fraught with economic depression, the devastating chestnut blight, a hog cholera epidemic, the worst drought in 100 years, and a smear campaign against an innocent people orchestrated by Park proponents and the media.

Roosevelt's entourage motored from Big Meadows to Farmington Country Club in Charlottesville. There the President spent the evening and night before speaking the following day, Saturday, July 4, at Thomas Jefferson's Monticello. His election campaign theme song, *Happy Days Are Here Again*, was doubtlessly played while he was in town, but it was probably not running through the minds of the former residents of the Blue Ridge Mountains in Monticello's western viewshed.

Today, descendants of Christopher Columbus Via bushwhack almost a mile down from Shenandoah National Park's Skyline Drive, carrying the tools needed to maintain their ancestral burial ground in Via Gap. They search the surrounding woods—some on private lands, some in the Park—to pay homage at the home sites of their mountain ancestors. Similar pilgrimages are repeated throughout the Park by other families. They are occasionally accompanied by one who can still recall the days before the families were scattered and the mountain lands provided all of their needs.

It is their legacy and sacrifice that we honor with our appreciation and respect for the lands they once called home.

Large advertising broadsides such as this 1951 movie poster were routinely posted around western Albemarle County. Crozet Theatre helped to anchor the downtown area as a destination for shopping and entertainment.

27

The Crozet Theatre

Mac Sandridge photographed the interior of Crozet Theatre when he was working there as projectionist during his 1948-49 senior year at Crozet High School. The theater had been refurbished after having suffered extensive fire damage.

Crozet's former downtown cold storage building was renovated in 1980 to create Windham, now Mountainside Senior Living. During that time, several other landmark Main Street buildings were razed, forever altering the visual character of this historic village. The Bank of Crozet edifice, admired by many as the grandest building in town, was lost to the ages. Adjacent to the Cold Storage, a much plainer structure was lost that may have been downtown Crozet's most memory-filled building.

A mention of the Crozet Theatre to anyone who attended its shows or worked there always elicits special memories of a time when Crozet was the commercial and social hub for western Albemarle County.

"That theater had a lot of history to it," stated Bob Crickenberger. "At one time it was the only form of recreation in town. It was a big thing."

The theater building was originally home to Haden Bros. general mercantile business. When brothers C. J. and C. A. purchased the property near Crozet Depot from James and Maggie Jarman, it was described in the 1897 deed as "the remainder of [Jarman's] orchard." The brothers'

ADMIT   **O N E**

Children's Christmas Show

CROZET THEATRE

Wednesday, December 10, 1958 - 7:00 P. M.

————————COMPLIMENTS————————

Red Front Five and Ten

Nannie Wagner's Red Front Five and Ten, located on The Square, featured a retail Toy Land during the Christmas shopping season. Along with her husband, Jack, who operated the Red Front Grocery next door, she helped to sponsor and promote a special Christmas show at Crozet Theatre. [Courtesy of Crozet Print Shop.]

original wood-framed structure was rebuilt as a cement block building in 1910, two years before William Carter began construction of his massive cold storage facility between their store and the C&O tracks.

Bill Haden, son of Curtis A. Haden, renovated his father's store into a movie theater in 1938, naming his new enterprise the Crozet Theatre. Among his first employees was young Bob Crickenberger.

"I started out delivering handbills on my bicycle," Crickenberger recalled. "I got ten cents a day—enough to go to the movies. Then I started taking up tickets, and, later, selling tickets. Charlie Smith was up in the projection booth and he taught me how to run the projectors. When he went into the [military] service, I took it over."

During its years of operation, many in the theater's workforce were eager students from Crozet High School. Different theater employee names are remembered depending on which high school graduating class one speaks with. Oftentimes it was the trusted older high school students who managed the theater.

In addition to motion pictures, live stage acts occasionally were featured. Country music stars of *The Grand Ol' Opry* as well as members of Richmond, Virginia's *Old Dominion Barn Dance* wound their way through Crozet. The theater's stage showcased performers like Sunshine Sue,

This c.1911 view from The Square in downtown Crozet includes the original Bank of Crozet with its four stately white columns. Curtis Haden's store, directly across Main Street from the Drug Store, was converted to Crozet Theatre in 1938.

Maybelle Carter and the Carter Sisters, Little Jimmie Dickens and a host of others, including local musician Billy Vest.

In the 1970s, music historian Clivis Harris of Charlottesville interviewed Afton/Greenwood native Billy Vest at Vest's home in Crozet. Vest, who sometimes billed himself as "The Strolling Yodler", had obtained a good measure of musical success in the early 1930s, traveling and appearing with Jimmie Rodgers, one of country music's first superstars. Vest also traveled the country with his own band and enjoyed some singing parts in films with Gene Autry in the 1940s and '50s.

"I know a lot of my records have sold here in this part of the country," he recounted. "In fact, right here at Crozet, at the hardware—that used to be a theater—I played there seven times. Afternoon and night. Matinee and night. And every time that I played there I had that place packed and I had to give a second performance.

"Back in those days a lot of times I was solo and, what went on there was, I would play at intermission. In other words, if the films—and they always had the news—you remember that? If that lasted an hour and 45 minutes, well then, I'd pick up 15 minutes on stage. They had a Hoot Gibson film on, and I was hired by this outfit in California to follow this film. In other words, I was advance man, publicity agent. I would take up 15 minutes or 20 minutes, ever what it was like in the film. They had done cut the film and I would just go in and fill that up—with a guitar and singing. Just me. I had some very good chances back in those days."

By the late 1950s, attendance at Crozet Theatre had waned and the number of movie nights was reduced. The screen curtains were pulled closed for the last time around 1961. A competitor to Vivian and Pete McCauley's Modern Barber Shop soon set up for business in the theater's

Several vintage buildings were demolished along Crozet's Main Street in 1980 during a downtown renovation that featured the creation of the present-day Mountainside Senior Living facility. Crozet Hardware was the last occupant of the former Haden Store/Crozet Theatre building, seen in this photo yielding to a battering ram.

lobby, but the venture was short-lived.

Blue Ridge Boat Sales established a showroom in the theater's sloped auditorium in the mid-60s but it, too, was relatively short-lived. Local businessman Norman Gillum purchased the theater property from the Smith family in 1967. Following extensive renovations, he moved his Crozet Hardware business there. The former movie theater building was finally razed in 1980 to make way for Windham.

Movies, cartoons, newsreels, beauty pageants, live musical performers—even a stage show featuring an elderly man who claimed to be the outlaw Jesse James—those events and others entertained the area's citizens for portions of four decades.

A special memory was related of two brothers attending a Christmas "Kiddie Show" at Crozet Theatre in the late 1950s. The older brother Warren had been appointed to accompany his much younger sibling on the short walk from their house on Railroad Avenue to the special holiday season event. Following cartoons and a movie, all of the youngsters in the theater rushed toward the small lobby where it was rumored Santa Claus would be waiting.

The surge of kids and their companions slowed as Santa and his assistant were overwhelmed with the noisy, swarming crowd. As the line inched forward it became obvious that Santa wasn't going to be having any extended conversations because he was too busy handing out candy canes and other favors.

While studying the scene ahead, the younger brother became aware of something else: This was *not* the "real" Santa Claus (whom he had seen previously that month at the Sears & Roebuck store on Main Street in Charlottesville.) This was apparently one of those Santa "helpers" he had heard about. Plus… this Santa had dark green eyes—remarkably like those of his older brother Meredith. Warren, shuffling alongside his little brother, had not let on (for some strange reason) that he had also noticed the similarity. As they got closer, the youngest brother began to call out, "Hi Meredith! I know you. You're Meredith. Hi, Meredith!"

"Santa" didn't extend good tidings to the brothers that night, but as the familiar green eyes glanced their direction, his assistant quickly passed along the boys' holiday favors before they headed outside.

It's not known exactly what the boys talked about on their walk back home that evening, but it was related that when Christmas morning finally rolled around, Santa had left just enough items from the youngest brother's Christmas wish-list to indicate there'd been no permanent damage to any relationships that exciting evening at the Crozet Theatre.

Western Albemarle County native Billy Vest toured the country, singing and yodeling his popular style of country music from the late 1920s until the early 1950s. He performed at Crozet Theatre several times. [Photo courtesy of the Viar family.]

28
Sallie Shoestring

AT F.U.H.S. 1926.   BELLE

Belle Dunn's school days began in 1923 at Free Union High School. [Photo courtesy of the Dunn-Bing Collection.]

Sallie Shoestring was the genuine article, and her life of 93 years is still recalled by the many who are her legacy.

Shoestring, of course, wasn't her real name, and neither was Sallie. But it was bestowed upon her at an early age by a group quite representative of the many groups to whom she would spend her life in service.

Isabelle Dunn—Belle to her family and friends—was born in the early fall of 1916 on her family's farm out in the country near Free Union. Her grandfather Thomas M. Dunn was that area's physician for 60 years. The youngest of five siblings and two half-siblings, she often related that her first nickname, Nuisance, was given by her dearest half-brother.

"I lived on a farm all my growing up years and much later," she recalled. "Farm life was busy but we enjoyed the work and play. My mother died when I was about 2½ years old. My father raised us. We never lacked for food or clothing. It may not have been the best but it was what Dad could afford."

The first five years of Belle's elementary schooling were at Free Union High School. Her sister

The old Dunn Homeplace near Free Union. [Photo courtesy of the Dunn-Bing Collection.]

Sarah began her own teaching career in 1928 at nearby Flint Hill School. There, Sarah had the rare opportunity of teaching her younger sister during Belle's sixth and seventh grade years.

Flint Hill, where *all* the students walked to school, was typical of small one-room schools far out in the country: a flat top stove in the center of the room, a painted green wall for a blackboard, a platform for the teacher's desk, drinking water carried by the boys from a nearby spring, and outside toilets. Sixth grade classes included reading, spelling, geography, history, civics, hygiene, arithmetic, handwriting and agriculture. Discipline was seldom needed but included standing in the corner or staying in during recess and writing sentences.

Lunches, often a cold biscuit with some meat and a cooked sweet potato, were carried in tin buckets and shared with students who had none. Recess and fun activities

Isabelle Dunn was the popular President of the Senior Class of 1934 at Meriwether Lewis High School. [Photo courtesy of the Dunn-Bing Collection.]

included "Annie Over the Schoolhouse," circle games and genuine "field" trips that were taken afoot.

The camaraderie among the school's 26 or so students led to almost everyone getting tagged with a nickname, including: Little Annie and Betty Jane (both boys), Muley, Pet, Runt, Sis, Sprout—and Sallie Shoestring.

It was from this arena of good basic education that the groundwork was laid for Flint Hill's "Sallie" to become the beloved school teacher she is revered as today.

Belle graduated in 1934 from Meriwether Lewis High School at Ivy. She was president of her senior class and christened the "Most Generous Girl" by her classmates. As did her sister Sarah, Belle obtained her teaching degree from Madison College in Harrisonburg.

Midway School, on the road between Crozet and Miller School, was her first teaching assignment in 1938. Her situation was nearly identical to her sister's experiences ten years earlier at Flint Hill, except water was carried from a neighbor's well, and she considered herself fortunate she had a real blackboard instead of a green-painted wall.

In this first teaching assignment, she roomed at a nearby home. She did not own a car, so she received permission to pasture her horse in the lot next to the house for the first part of the school year.

"That way I could go after school when and where I wanted to go," she said. "I couldn't get home fast enough to get saddled and be gone. It helped me to know the families, and I was able to visit homes often."

Belle Dunn Bing's 40-year teaching career included many years in the elementary schools at Greenwood and Crozet. Her teaching style was firm when necessary, but also light-hearted, animated and fun. From enduring a classroom of kids howling with laughter while she read aloud the antics of Miss Minerva, to shedding a tear with the class during a equally sad tale, she was able to teach so much more than just the 3 Rs. Kickball games in the school field were great fun; rainy days often brought out the record player and square dance records. Students' desks were pushed against the wall and the dreaded (by some) boy-girl pairings made for many awkward moments. Whew!

Sisters Sarah Dunn (left) and Isabelle Dunn Bing were well-known school teachers and active members of their community. [Photo courtesy of the Dunn-Bing Collection.]

Sixth-grader Sallie Shoestring and her horse Robin after classes at Flint Hill School. [[Photo courtesy of the Dunn-Bing Collection.]

This writer has long-credited his own love for history to Mrs. Bing's 4th-grade *Virginia History* class in 1961-62. Exciting stories of Captain John Smith in the 1600s were followed up with a bus trip to Jamestown. The story of Colonial Governor Alexander Spotswood's Knights of the Golden Horseshoe ascending the Blue Ridge Mountains seemed to bring the excitement of "ancient" history nearly to our Albemarle County doorsteps.

Automobile field trips to far-away places like Luray Caverns made opportunities for extended contests of counting cows. The miles were interspersed with sing-alongs from Mrs. Bing's bottomless repertoire of children's songs.

Little Sallie Shoestring absorbed the lessons she learned at home: lessons of hard work and well-deserved fun, respect for one's peers and for those in authority (even if it *is* your big sister); to these things she added her life experiences of love and loss and hard-fought victories; and she applied them all to energize and inspire those placed in her charge.

Isabelle Dunn Bing's life and legacy seem mirrored in a 1904 writing by Betty Anderson Stanley. Mrs. Bing saved a hand-written copy of the piece below with other inspirational writings.

Success In Life

"He has achieved success who has lived well, laughed often, and loved much; who has gained the respect of intelligent men and the love of little children; who has filled his niche and accomplished his task; who has left the world better than he found it, whether by an improved poppy, a perfect poem or a rescued soul; who has never lacked appreciation of earth's beauty or failed to express it; who has looked for the best in others and given the best he had; whose life was an inspiration; whose memory was a benediction."

Mrs. Bing's 4th grade class in 1957 at Greenwood Elementary School. [Photo courtesy of the Dunn-Bing Collection.]

John and Nora Rea with their first child, Margaret, c. 1908. Mr. Rea was a farmer and, later, Head Gardener at Miller Manual Labor School, before moving his family to Greenwood in 1924, where he was custodian and watchman at the high school. [Photo courtesy of the Rea family.]

29

Susie Pearle's Christmas Box

Standing on the front porch of her home, Little Greenwood, in 1928, Susie Pearle, second from right, is flanked by her cousin Martha Price, and her younger brothers John and Woodrow. Her mother Nora Rea holds the family's youngest, Carroll. [Photo courtesy of the Rea family.]

"I asked Mama one time why did she name me Pearle. I remember she looked at me real hard and said, 'Well, I thought it was pretty'. That's all she ever told me."

Susie Pearle Rea was born in 1918 at Critzer's Shop, Virginia, near Afton. She was the fourth daughter of tenant farmer John Erasmus "Ras" Rea and his young bride Nora Elizabeth, whose marriage had already endured the sadness of three stillborn infants. Four more children (another girl followed by three boys) were added to their family over the next ten years.

As was customary with tenant farming, Ras Rea's work included basic housing for his growing family. He had been taught the value of hard work by his father, Ryland, who had lost the use of his right arm when severely wounded during Pickett's Charge at Gettysburg in 1863.

Greenwood served as the backdrop for young Susie Pearle's formative years. Her father moved his family there in 1924 to assume the job of custodian for the *new* Greenwood High School which had been built during the 1921–'22 school year. Less demanding physically than the large-scale gardening he had done previously at Miller Manual Labor School, this custodial work provided the family with a place to live on the school grounds and convenient access to the village of

Greenwood.

"We would go across the road to McCue's field to play," said Susie Pearle. "The field was full of different trees, and it was a challenge, but I had to learn to climb every one of those trees. I can remember the old sycamore trees, when you would go up, the bark would come down, but you had to climb a tree.

"Sometimes I would make the walk up the road to Bruce's Store to pick up our mail at the post office in the store there near the depot. Box two-two [22]. That was our post office number the entire time we lived up there."

Susie Pearle's oldest sister Margaret had once attended school classes in the same building that later served as home for the Rea family. Margaret recalled: "Allie Critzer drove the wagon—it was a covered wagon—to Greenwood School when we lived up at Critzer's Shop. Coming back to [Route] 250 there's a long hill coming up through there. When there was snow on the ground, or it was raining and real muddy, everybody had to get off at the foot of the hill and walk to the top of the hill, and then get back on the bus.

"I rode from up there at Critzer's Shop to Greenwood School with a blanket over my lap and a lantern setting under there to keep my feet warm."

Margaret, Lucille, Ruby, Susie Pearle, Effie, John, Woodrow, Carroll — siblings all; born between 1907 and 1928. Christmas traditions in Ras and Nora's family evolved as family income fluctuated, as the family moved, and as the children grew up, married and moved away. Wild cedar trees were cut and adorned with both homemade and store-bought decorations: shiny balls

The house in the background was one in a succession of Greenwood, Virginia, schoolhouses used from 1889 until 1921 when the more modern two-story building, which still survives, was constructed. Affectionately referred to as Little Greenwood, this building, beginning in 1924, served as housing for the school's custodian. Susie Pearle, third from left, posed on the road out front with several of her siblings and cousins. [Photo courtesy of the Rea family.]

floated alongside paper dolls cut from news-print or butcher paper. Always, atop the tree, there was a star for the Christ Child, cut from cardboard and covered with tin foil.

"I never will forget—it was the first year I went to school," reminisced big sister Margaret. "[George S.] Gill's Store had the Christmas toys out. I would go and look at the different toys and I picked out a doll that I wanted. Every time I went I'd look at that doll. We believed in Santy Claus, you know. So I told them at home that I wanted that doll. Mama told me, 'Well, maybe you'll get it for Christmas.'

"Just before school was out for Christmas, I went up to the store and told old man Gill to put that doll away for Santy Claus to bring me. And he did. When Daddy went down there to buy his Christmas stuff, he asked him which of those dolls was it I had been looking at so much. Mr. Gill told him, 'Oh, I've got that one on lay-a-way for you.' Daddy said, '*What?*' Mr. Gill said, 'Yes, she came by here and told me to put it on lay-a-way.'

"And he wouldn't buy it for me. I got up Christmas morning thinking I was going to get that doll—and I got a doll—but I didn't get that one!"

Susie Pearle Rea's first grade photo at Greenwood High School in 1924. She always delighted in reciting the rhyme from the Baby Ray Primer lying open on the desk: "I see the moon and the moon sees me. God bless the moon and God bless me." [Photo courtesy of the Rea family.]

For Susie Pearle, memories of Christmas morning at home included rising early to see what Santa Claus had brought everyone. She remembered, too, that it was very important to get up at the same time as everyone else.

"Each of us had an open box with our name on it on Christmas morning, and all the boxes were lined up side-by-side along the wall," she recalled with a smile. "We would get some hard candy, an orange or apple, a hand full of nuts, and maybe a special toy or some other pretty.

"If you weren't right on time and got there a little later than the others, someone might sneak something out of your box and put it into theirs!"

The Christian values modeled by Ras and Nora Rea prevailed as their children grew. Following their father's passing early in 1932, all the children stepped up to help ensure their mother would continue to have a place to live and care for the siblings still at home. Those who had moved away

A comical postcard greeting from Greenwood, Virginia, c. 1915.

The proprietors at the mercantile adjacent to Greenwood High School in the 1920s and '30s minced no words in describing their wares.

for work regularly sent support money home. For several years, Nora and the children still at home labored together to perform Ras's custodial duties at the school, assuring themselves the continued privilege of a home on the Greenwood School property.

Susie Pearle graduated from high school a few years after her father passed away, while her family still lived at Little Greenwood. She married a year and a half later, just a few days before Christmas, and moved away from the Greenwood village. During her lifetime of 80+ years, she enjoyed the companionship of each of her siblings, nurtured a family of her own, and found continued joy by adding to the Christmas boxes of others.

Paul H. Cale served Greenwood High School as teacher, coach and principal from 1935-46. A respected mentor and community leader, he then served Albemarle County Schools in an administrative capacity until his retirement in 1969. In 1967, while Division Superintendent, he sent the following Christmas message to those teachers working under his charge. Believing Mr. Cale's sentiments bear repeating, this writer passes them along during this blessed Christmas season:

"Emerson said many years ago, 'The only true gift is a portion of thyself.' You are continually making this contribution as you go about your tasks.

"Is not this what Christmas is all about? For many, many years ago, we were told that 'God so loved the world that He gave His only begotten Son...' Although the finite mind cannot fathom such great love, through faith we know that Christmas commemorates the greatest gift, for Jesus said, 'I and My Father are one.' In sending His Son He gave Himself.

"May you and your loved ones experience during Christmas and throughout the coming year the joy, peace and well-being which attends those who have room in their lives for this greatest of gifts, the Prince of Peace."

Index

PHIL JAMES is a native of western Albemarle County, Virginia. Across four decades, he has researched and gathered the stories of the people and communities of the near-by Blue Ridge Mountains. Blending the oral histories he has collected along with photos copied from the family albums of his hosts, he presents the region's history within the context of the people who have lived it.

His award winning column, *Secrets of the Blue Ridge*, has appeared regularly in the *Crozet Gazette* since 2006. In addition to sharing his passion for local history with school and civic groups, he has taught university-level short courses through the Osher Lifelong Learning Institute at the University of Virginia.